ART NOUVEAU
DESIGNS COLORING BOOK

MARTY NOBLE

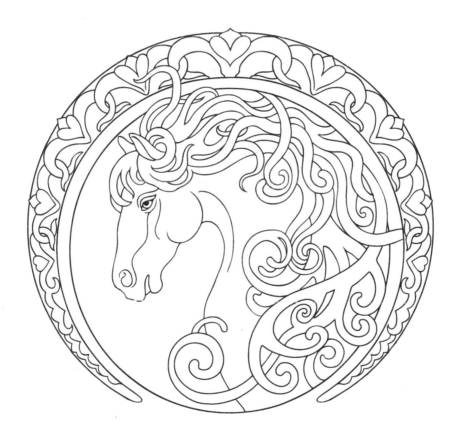

DOVER PUBLICATIONS, INC.
MINEOLA, NEW YORK

Bibliographical Note

Art Nouveau Designs Coloring Book contains all the plates from the following previously published Dover books by Marty Noble: *Art Nouveau Animal Designs* and *Art Nouveau Patterns*.

International Standard Book Number

ISBN-13: 978-0-486-80351-7
ISBN-10: 0-486-80351-1

Manufactured in the United States by RR Donnelley
80351104   2015
www.doverpublications.com

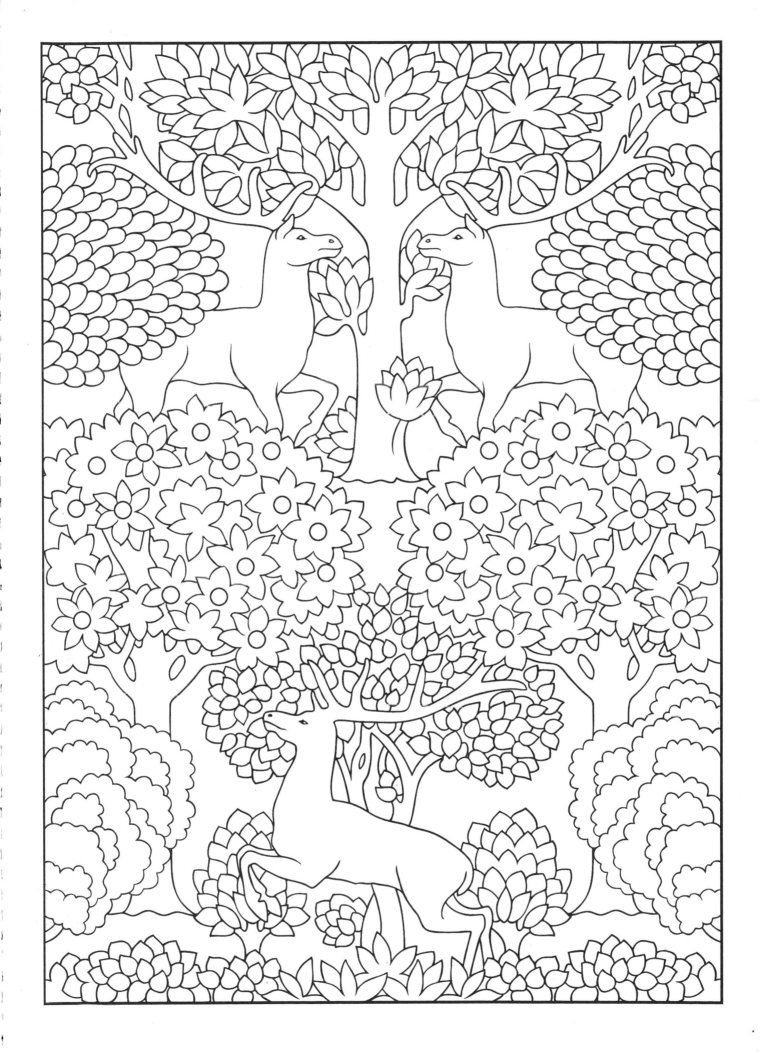

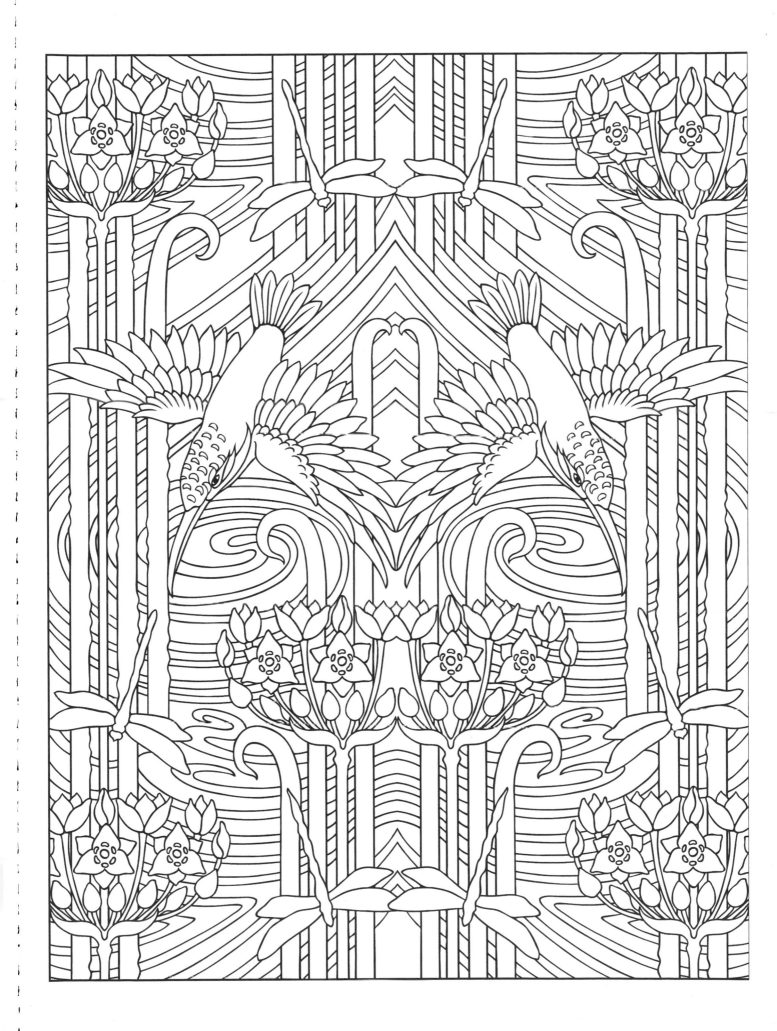

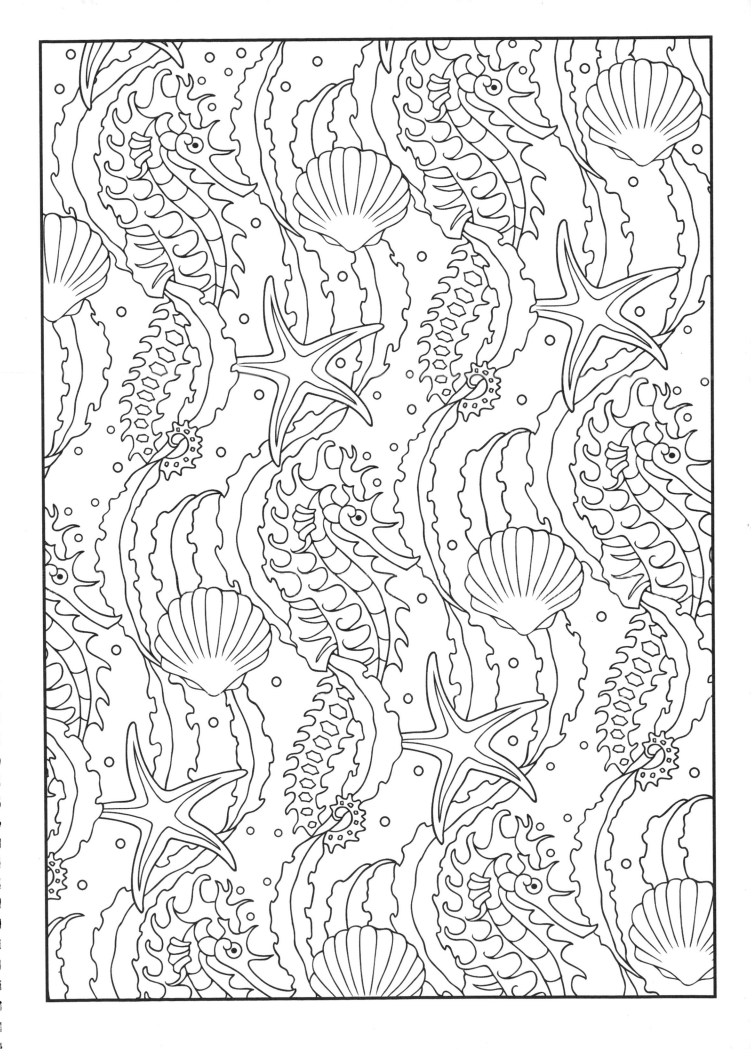

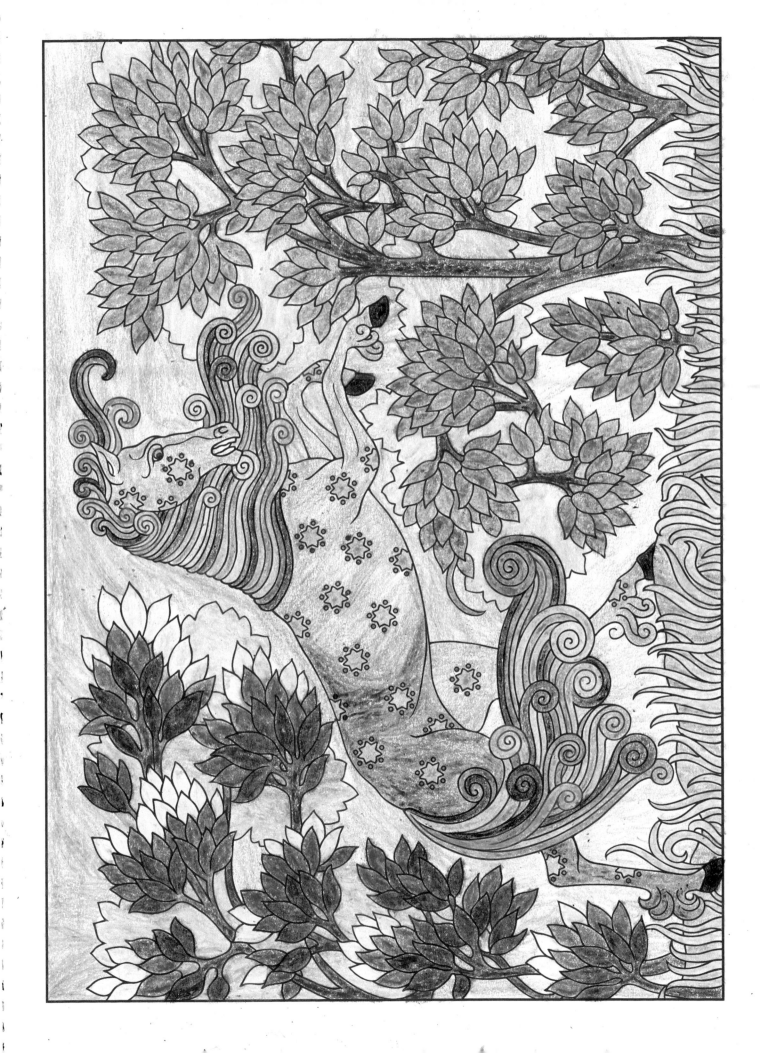

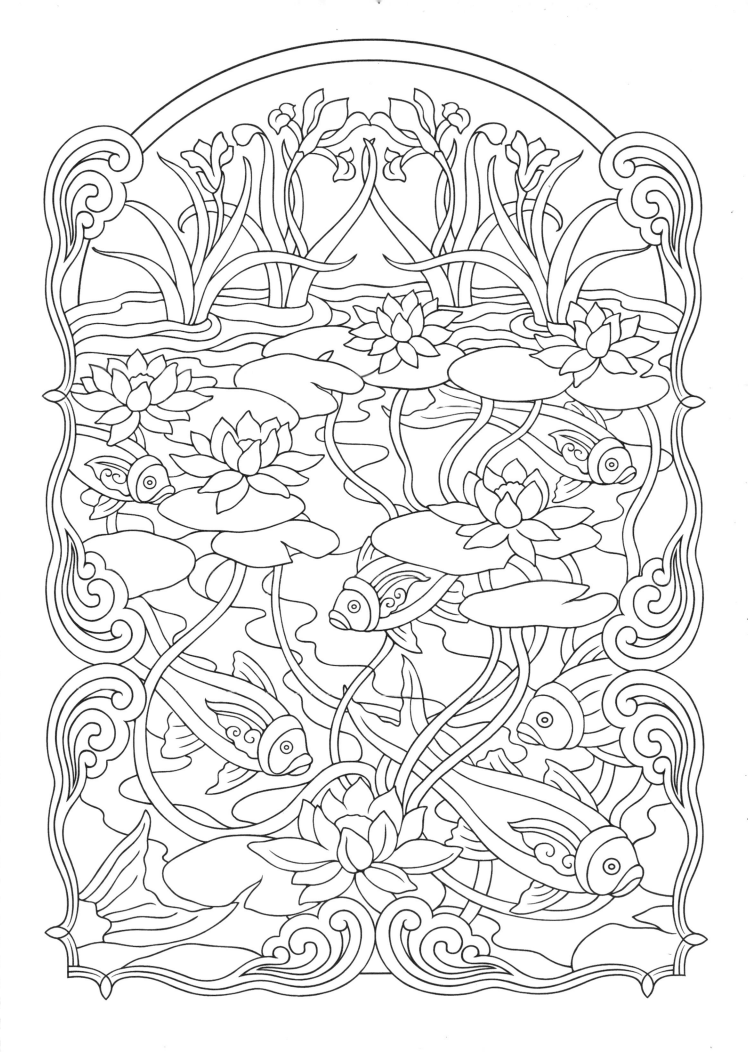

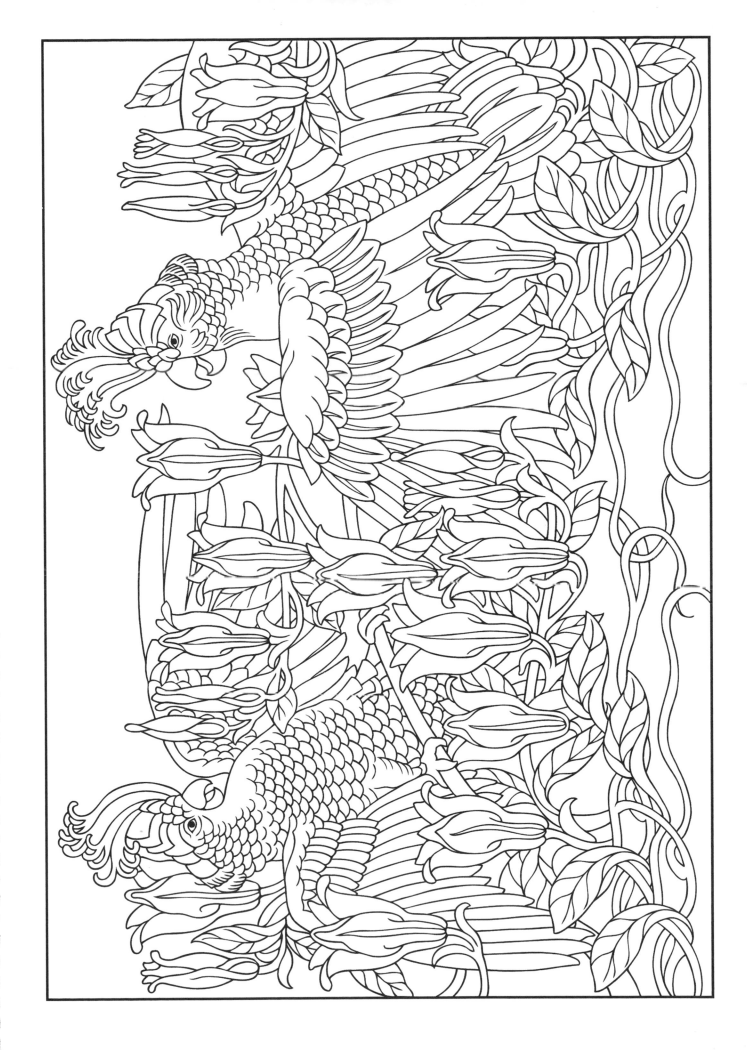

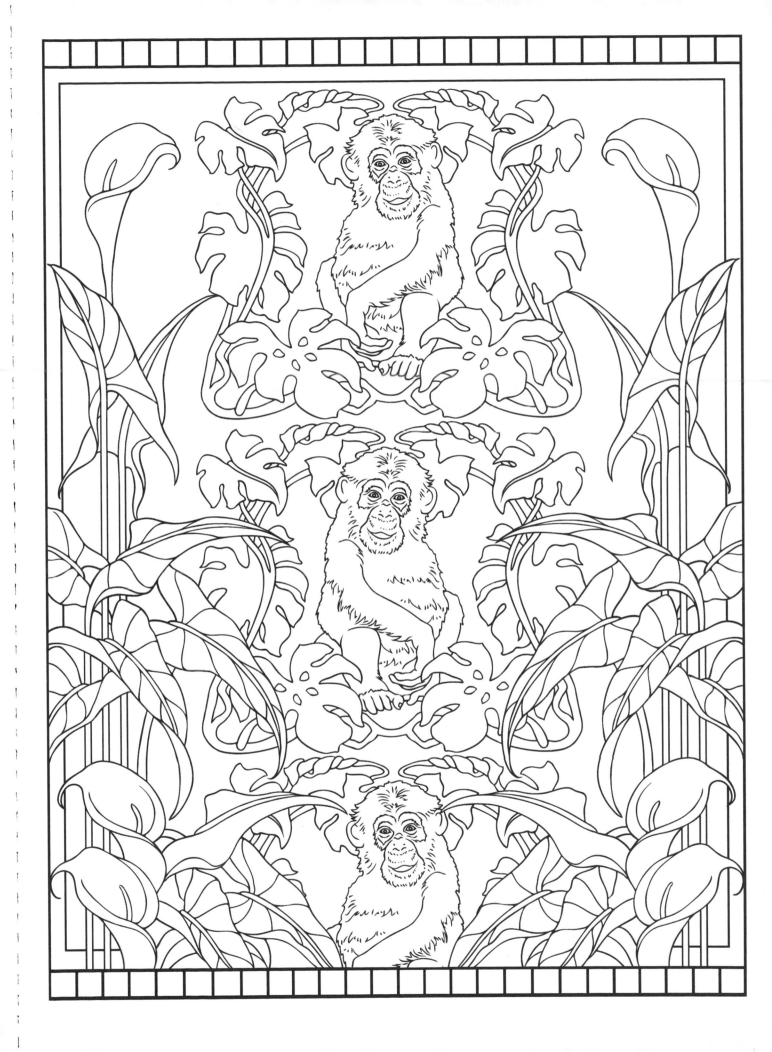

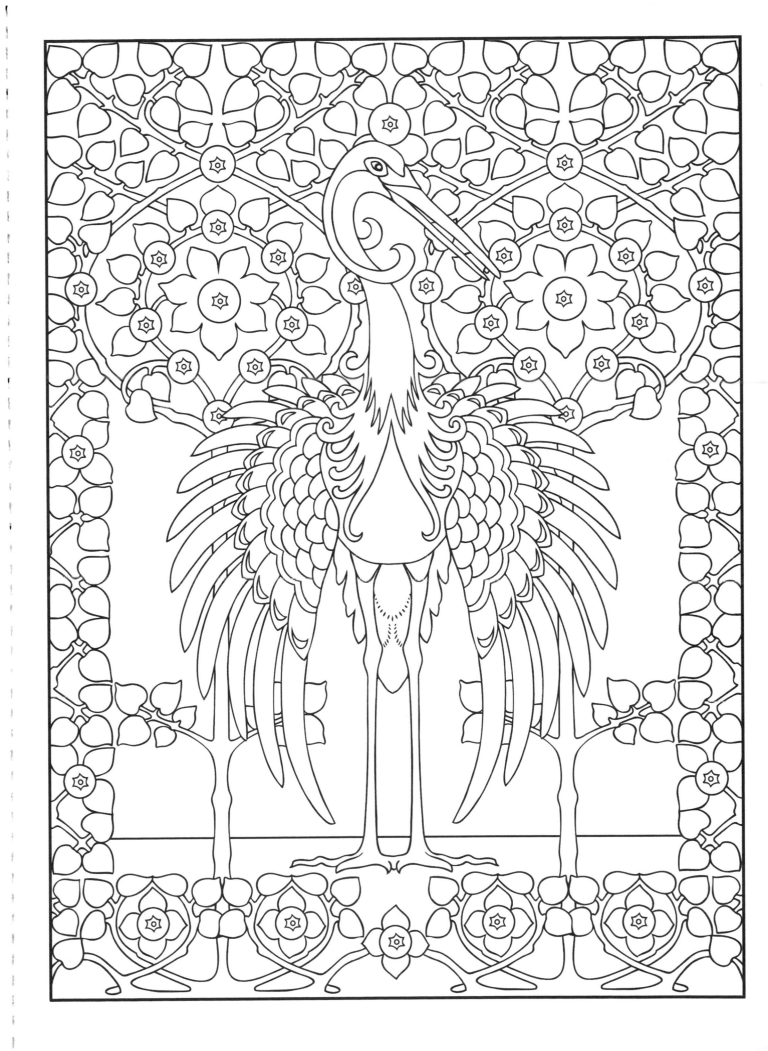

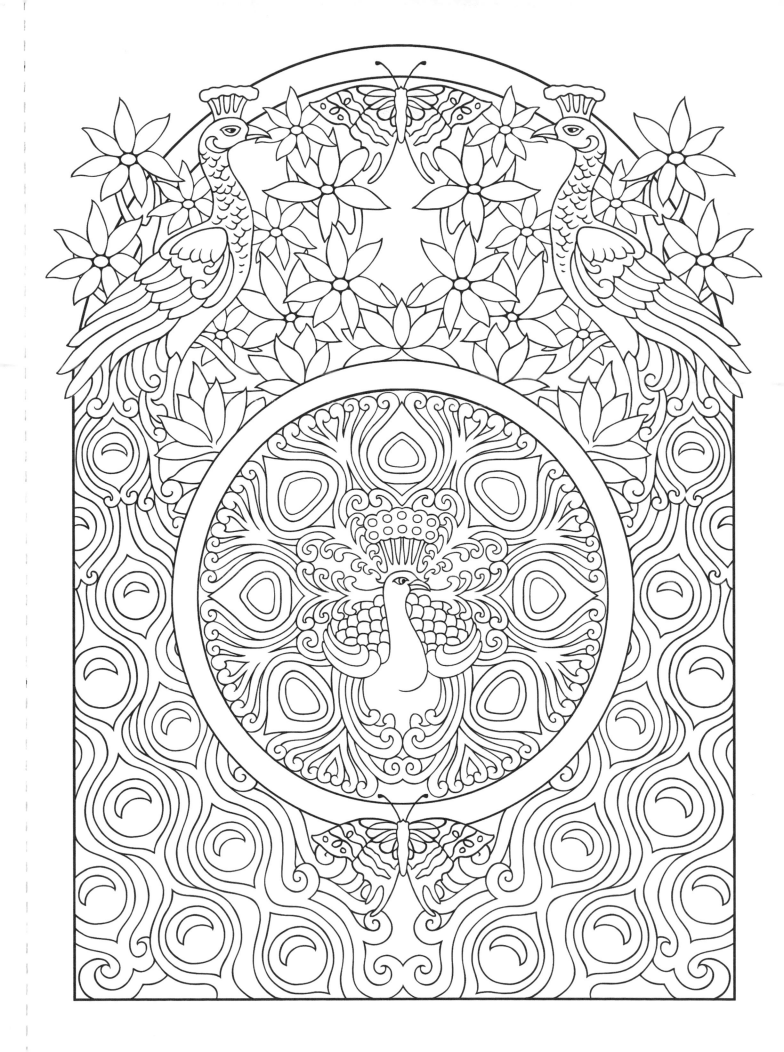

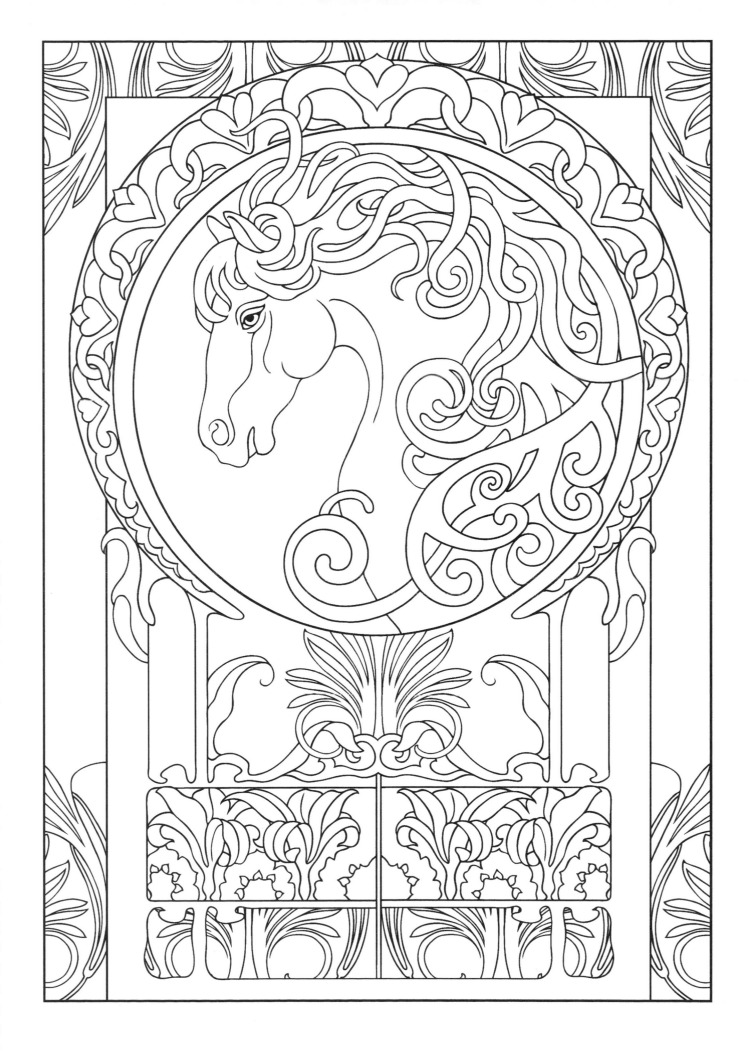

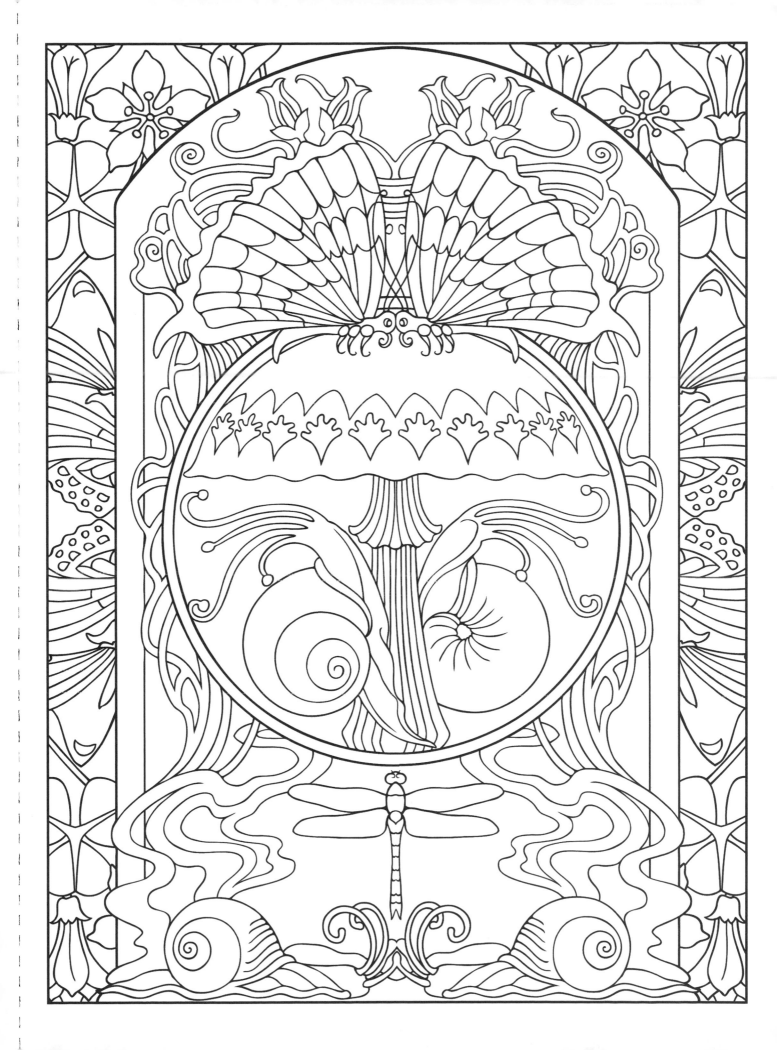

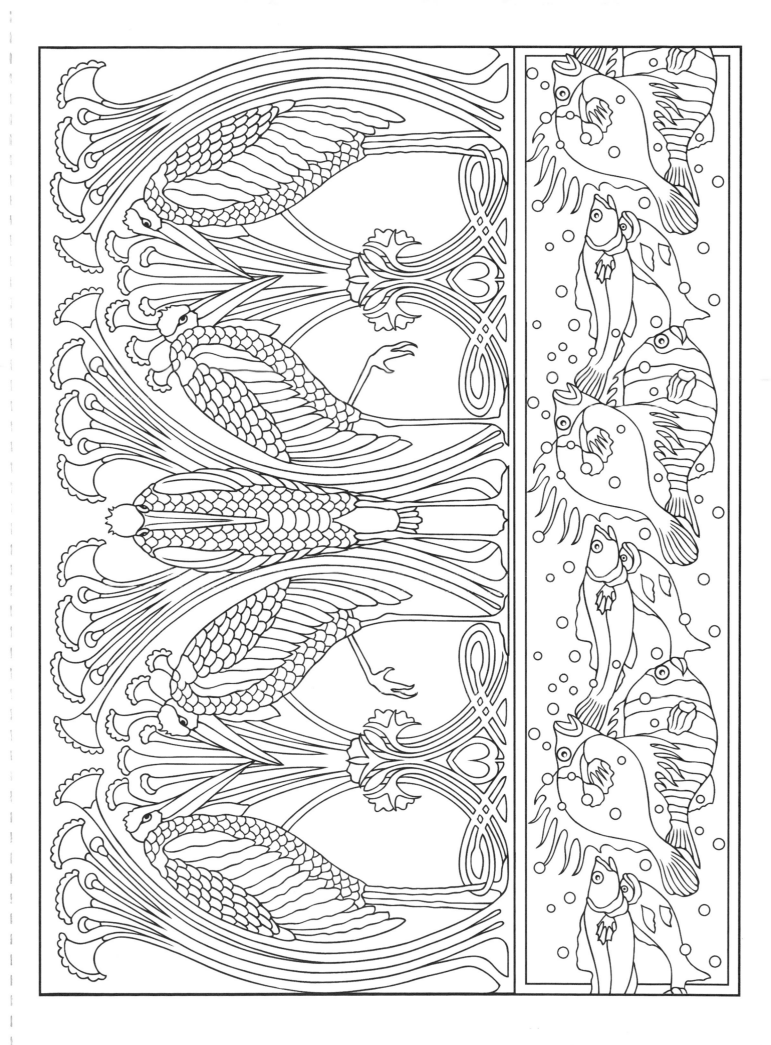

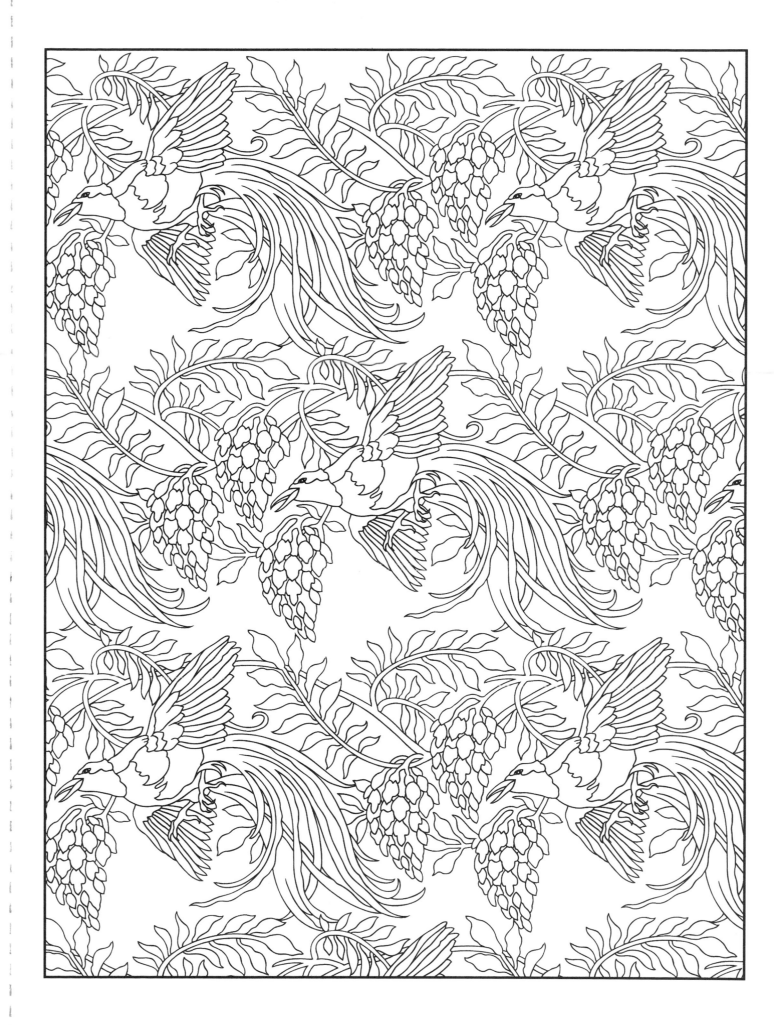

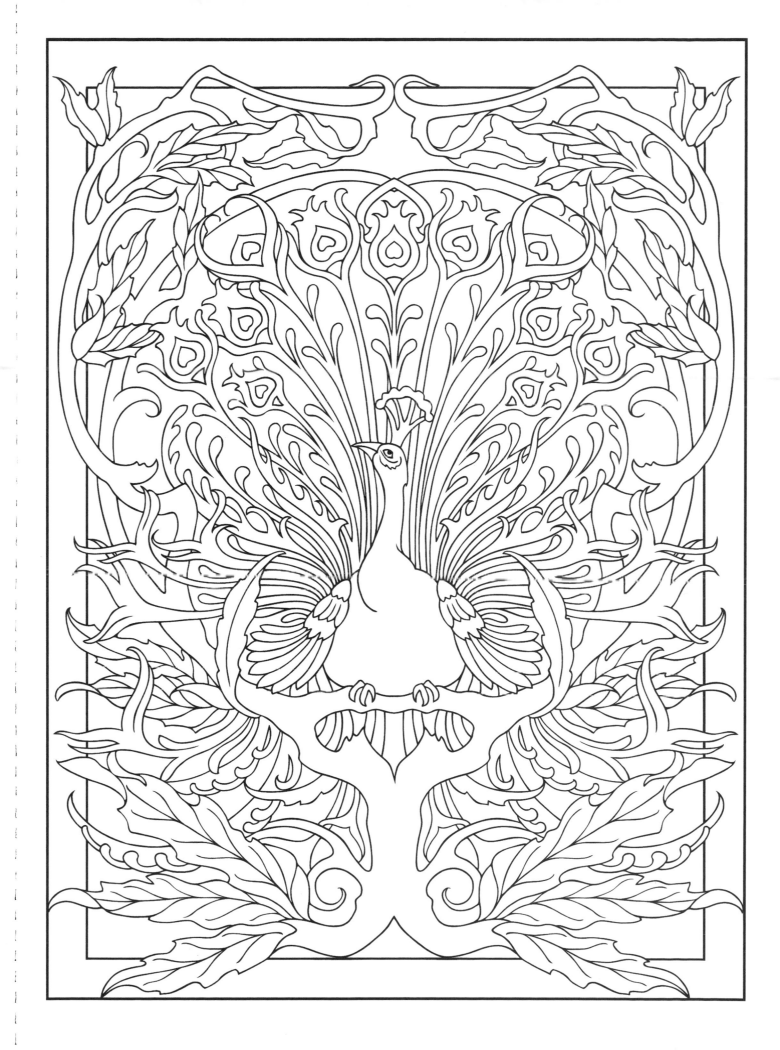

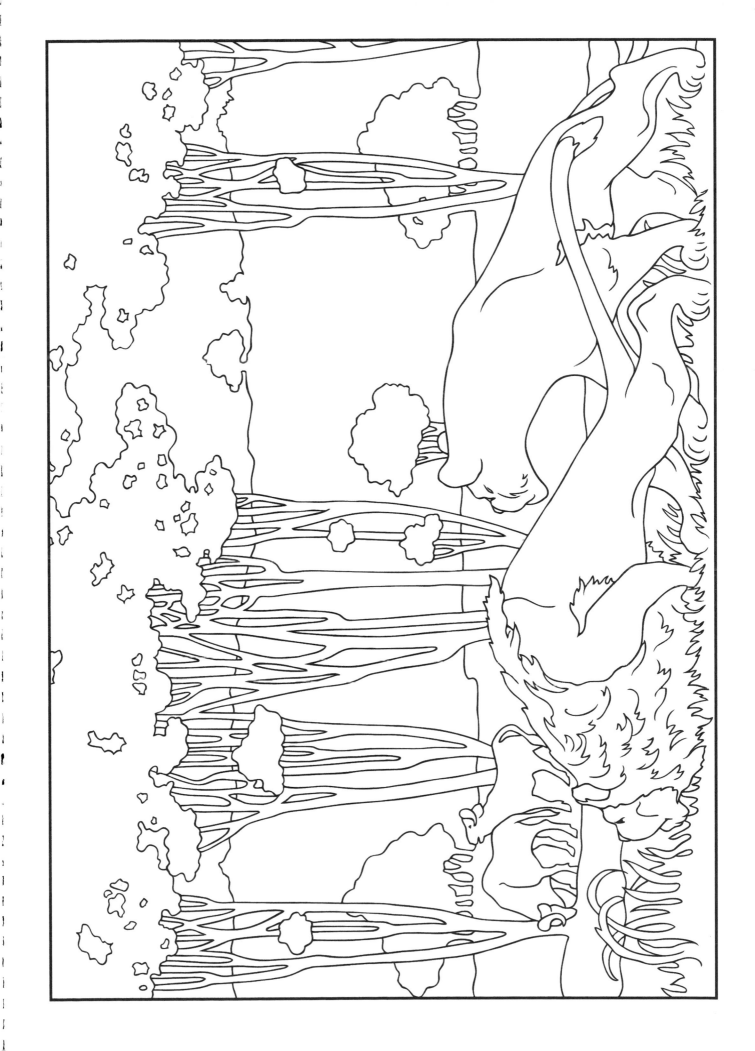

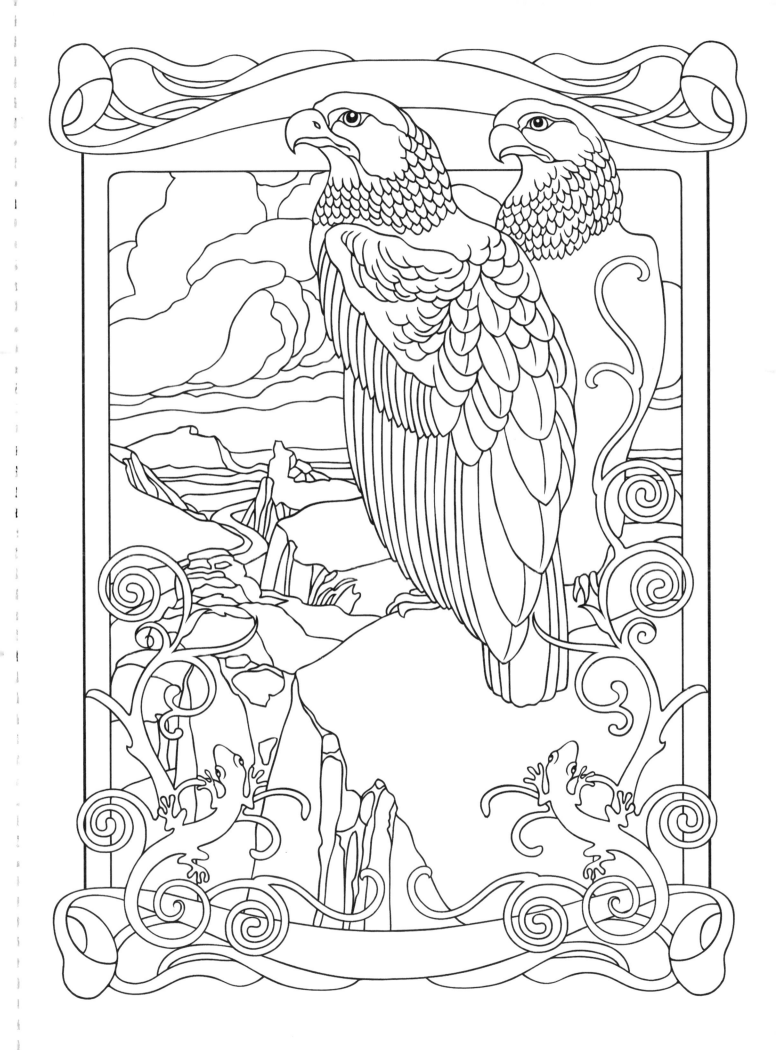

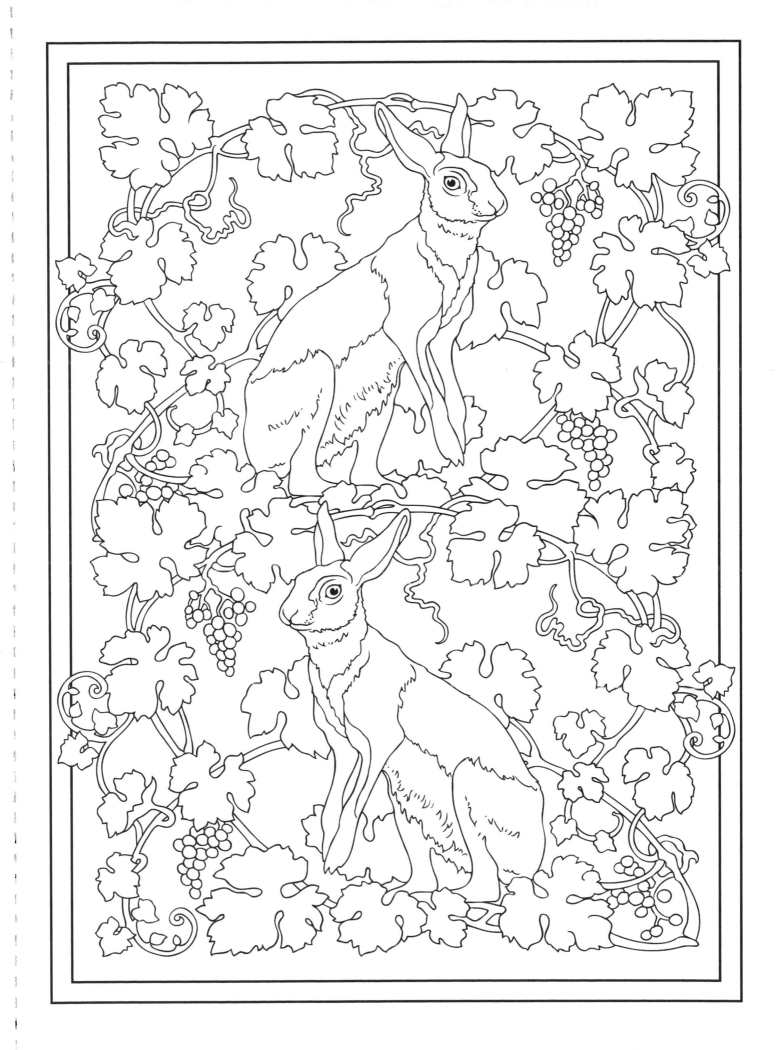

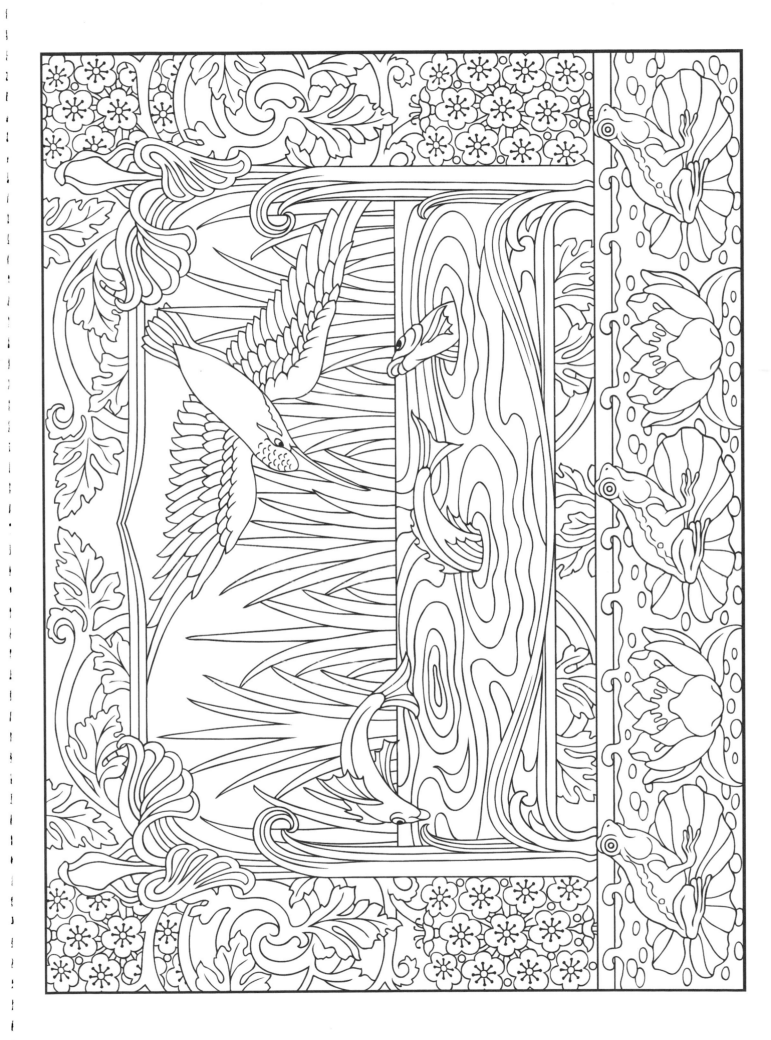

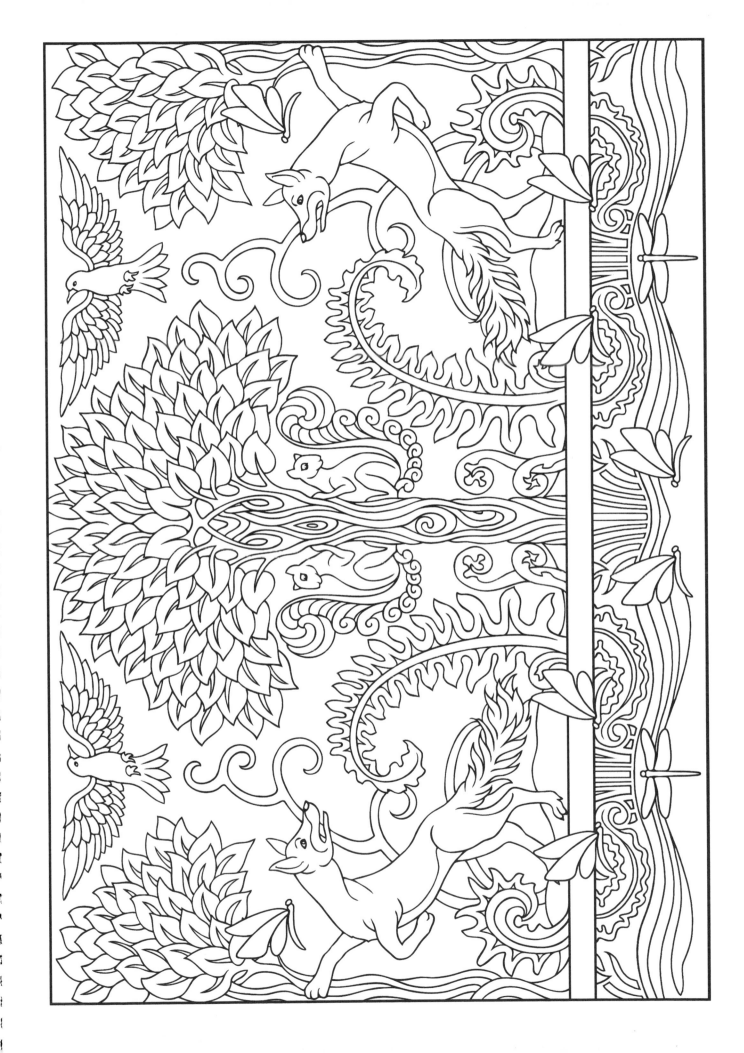

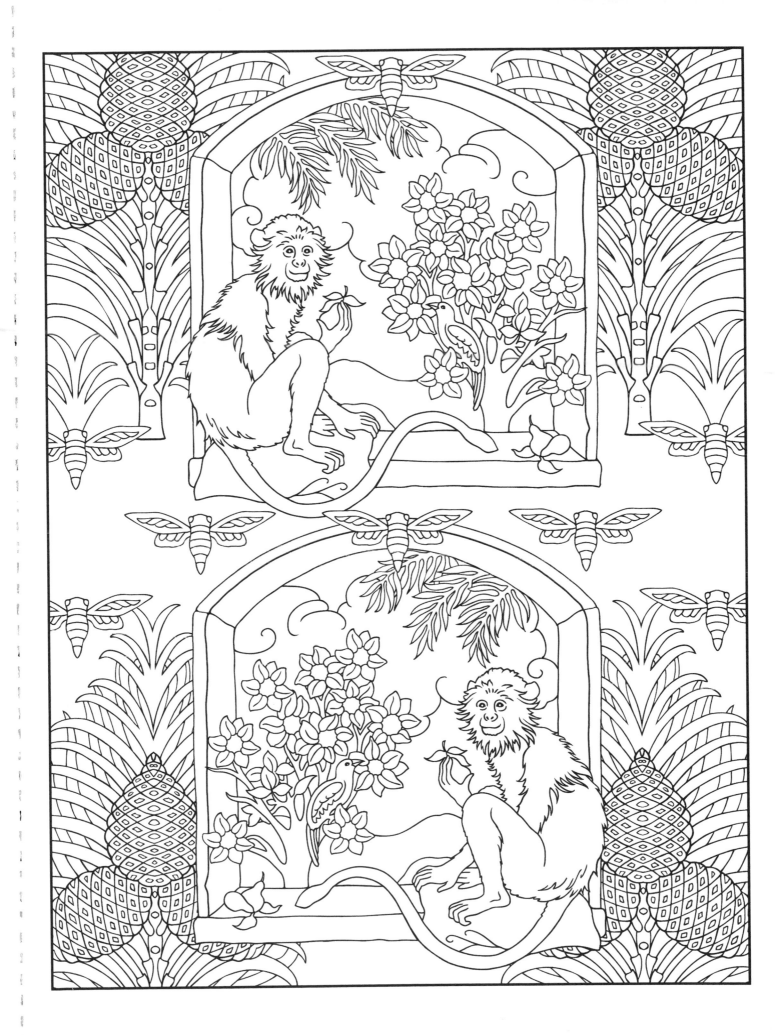

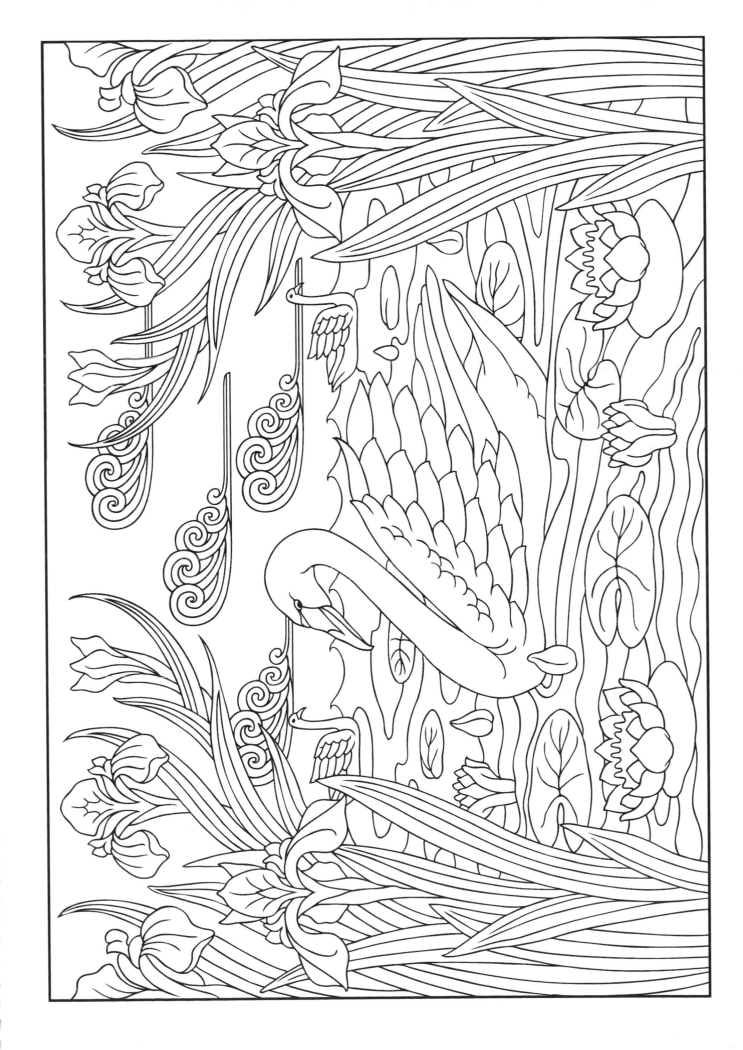

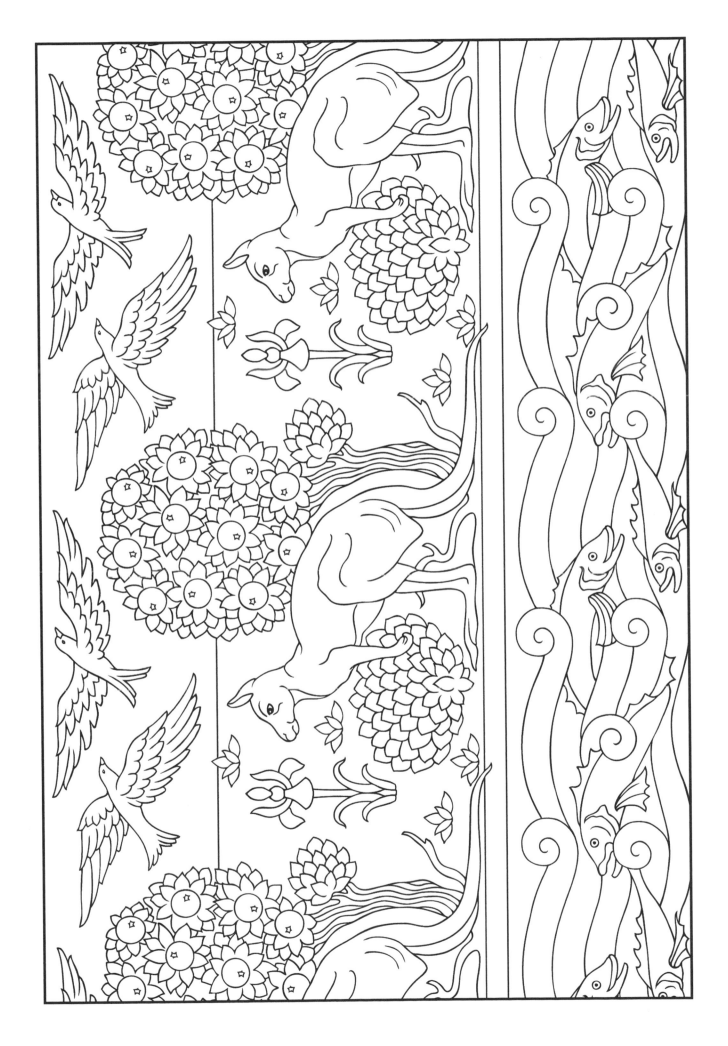

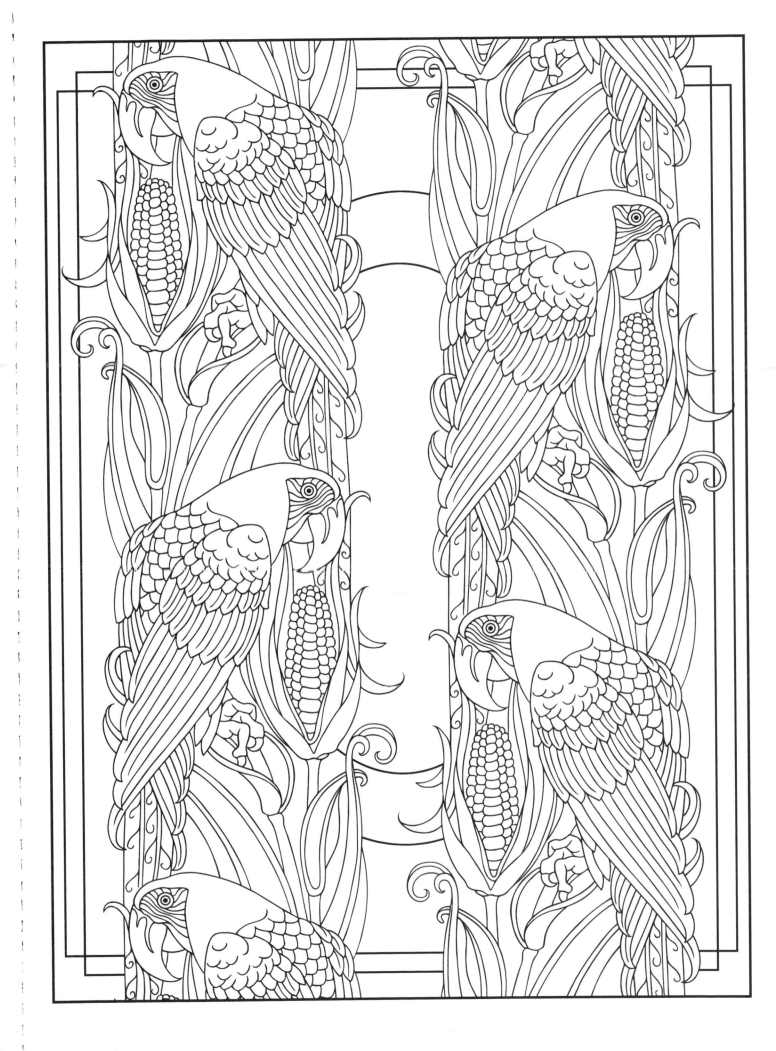

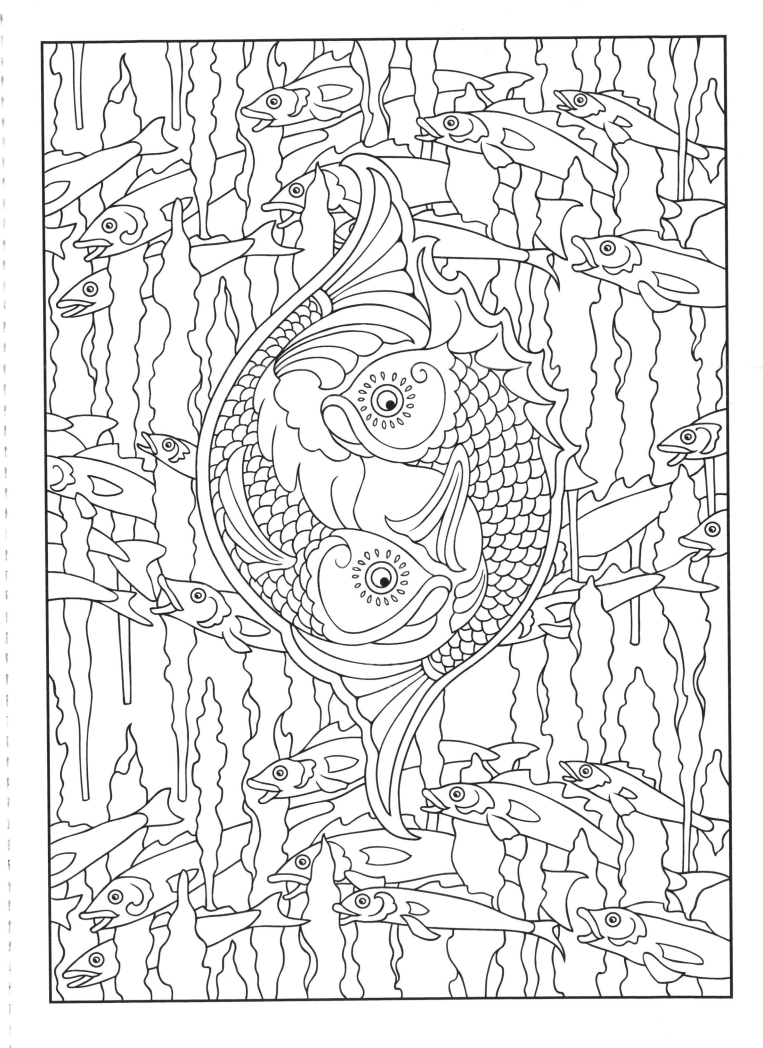

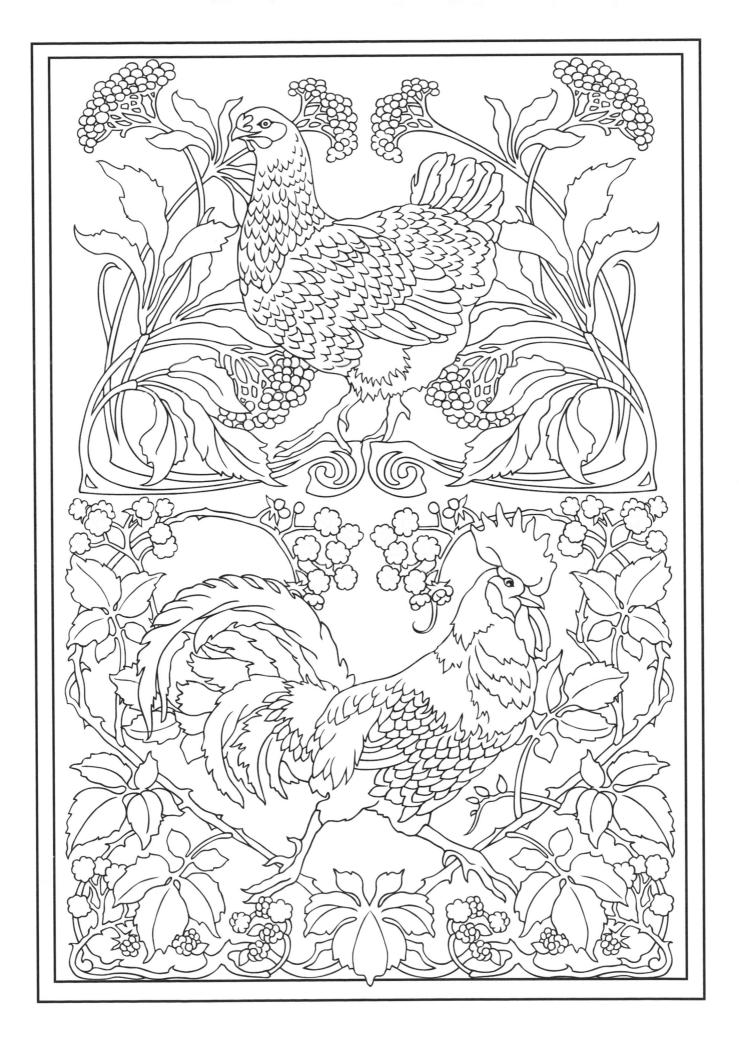

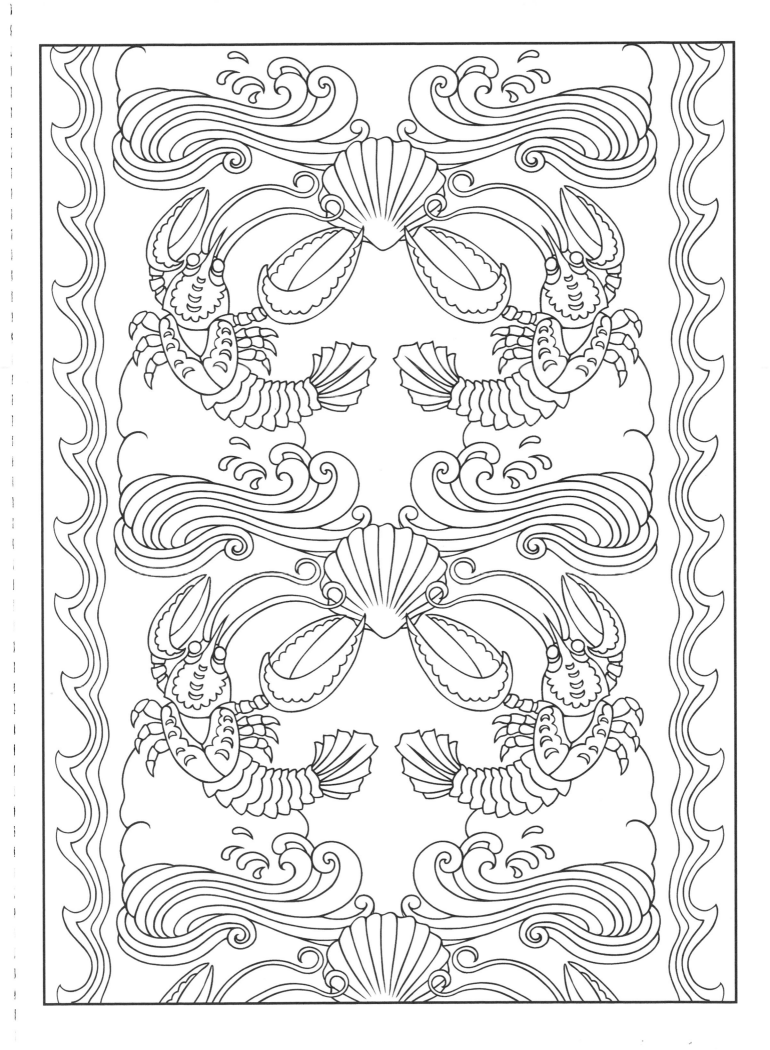

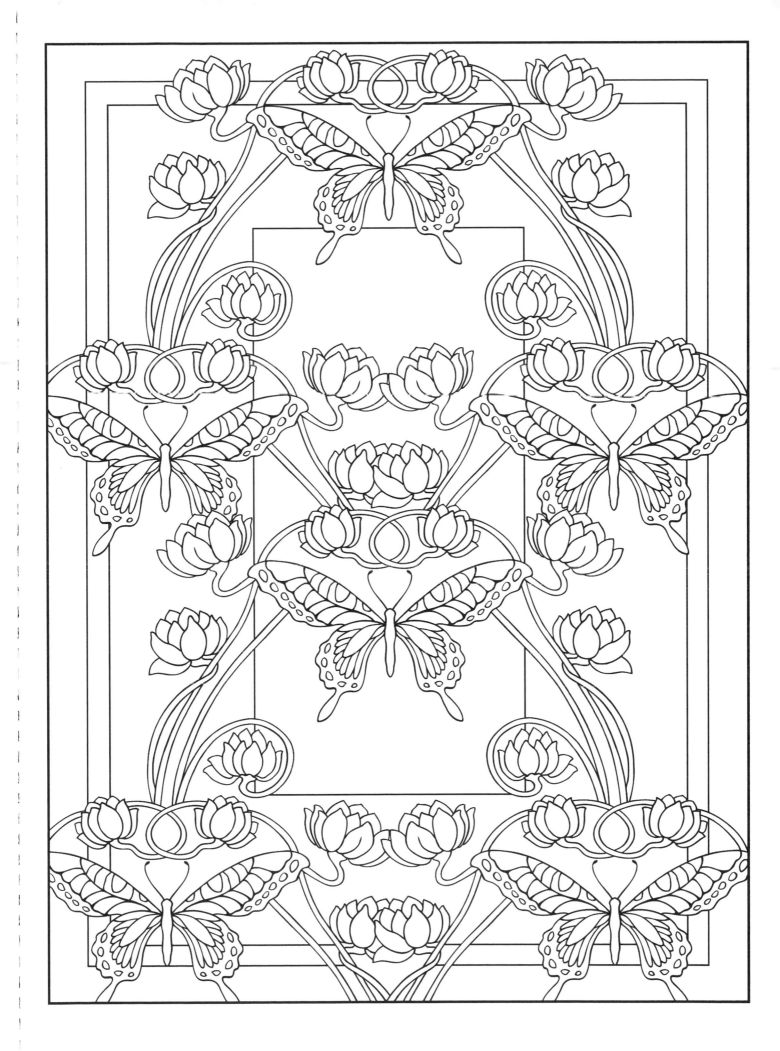

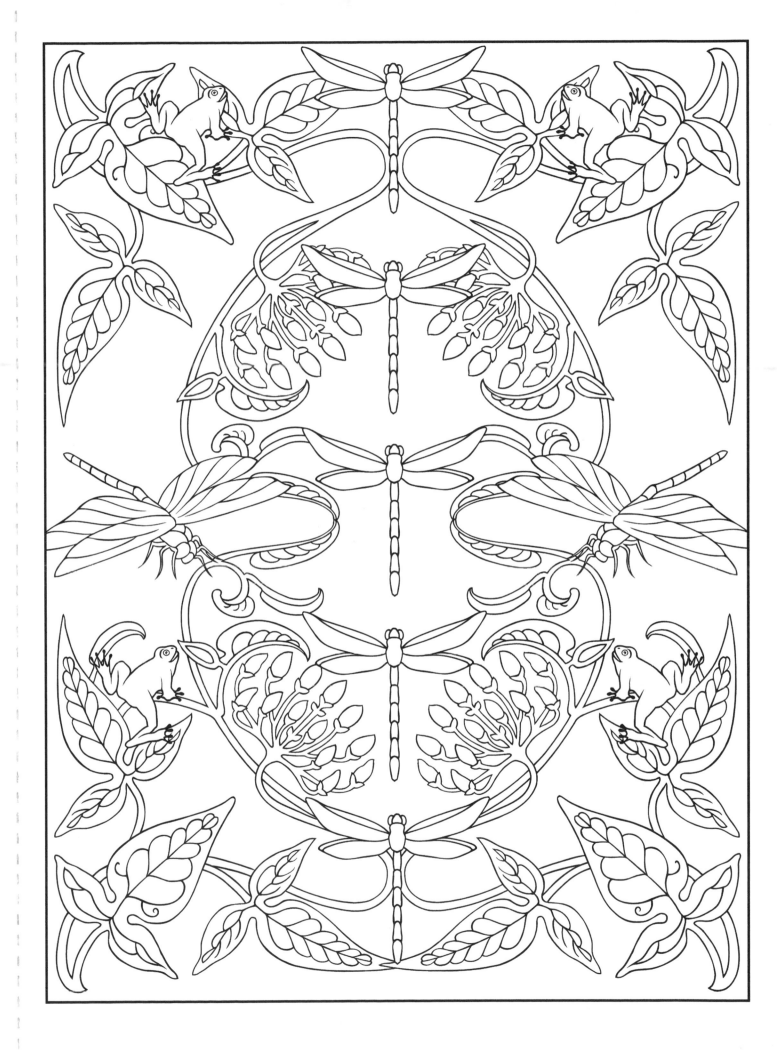

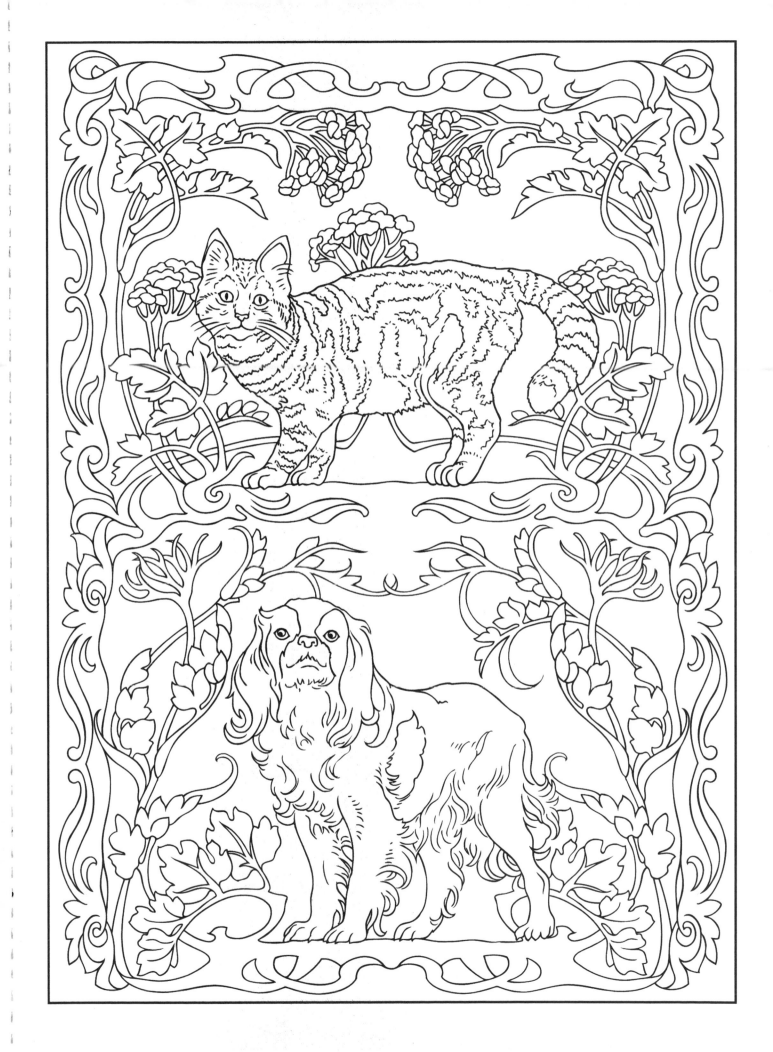

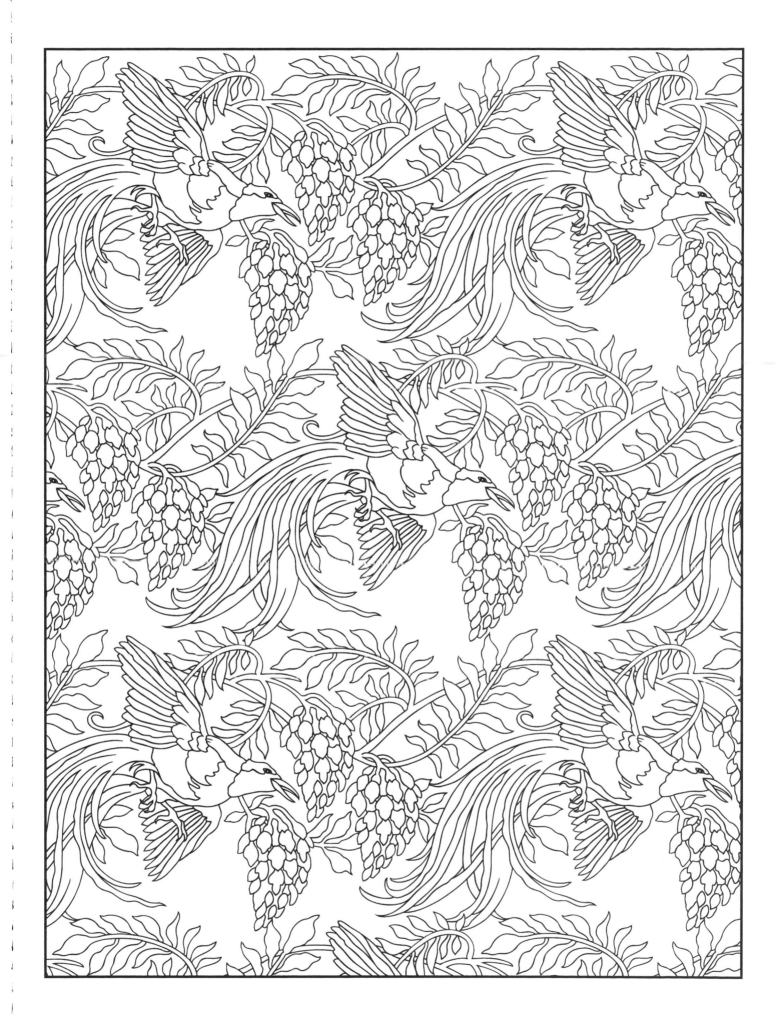

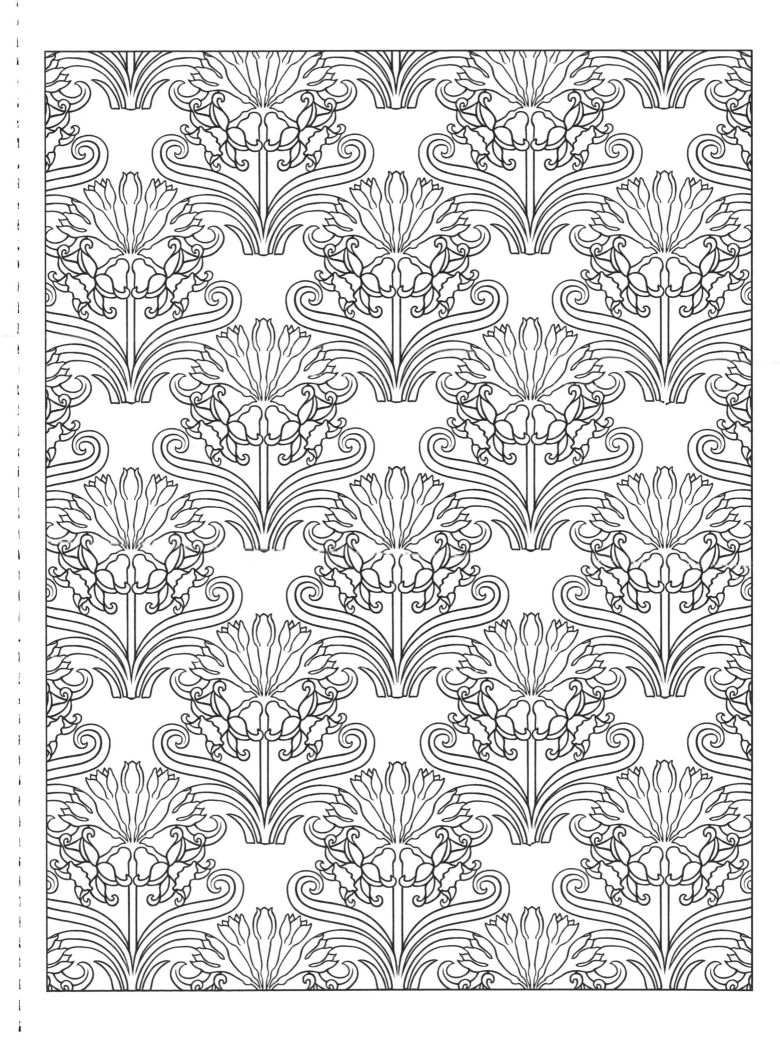

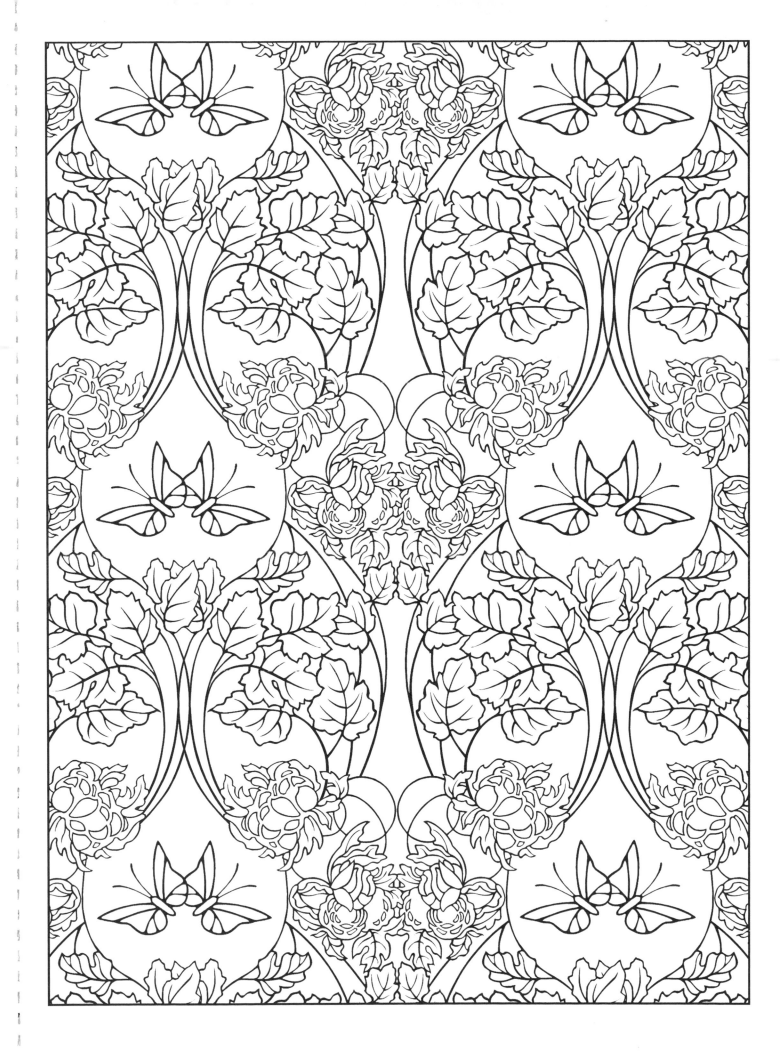

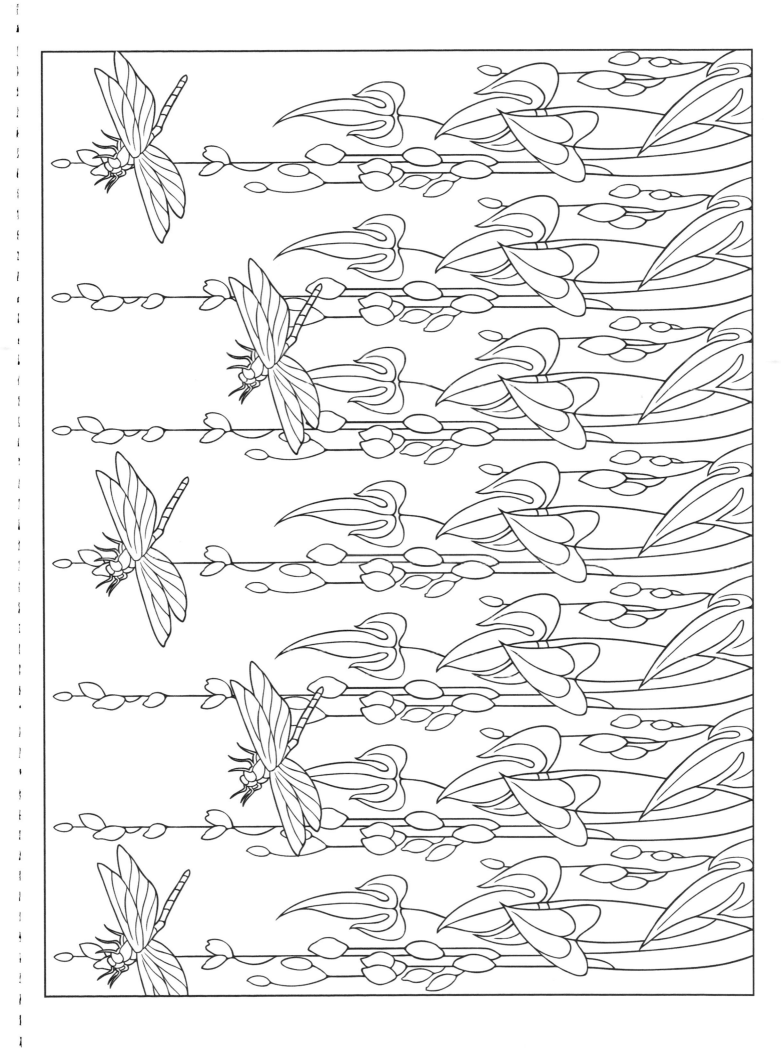

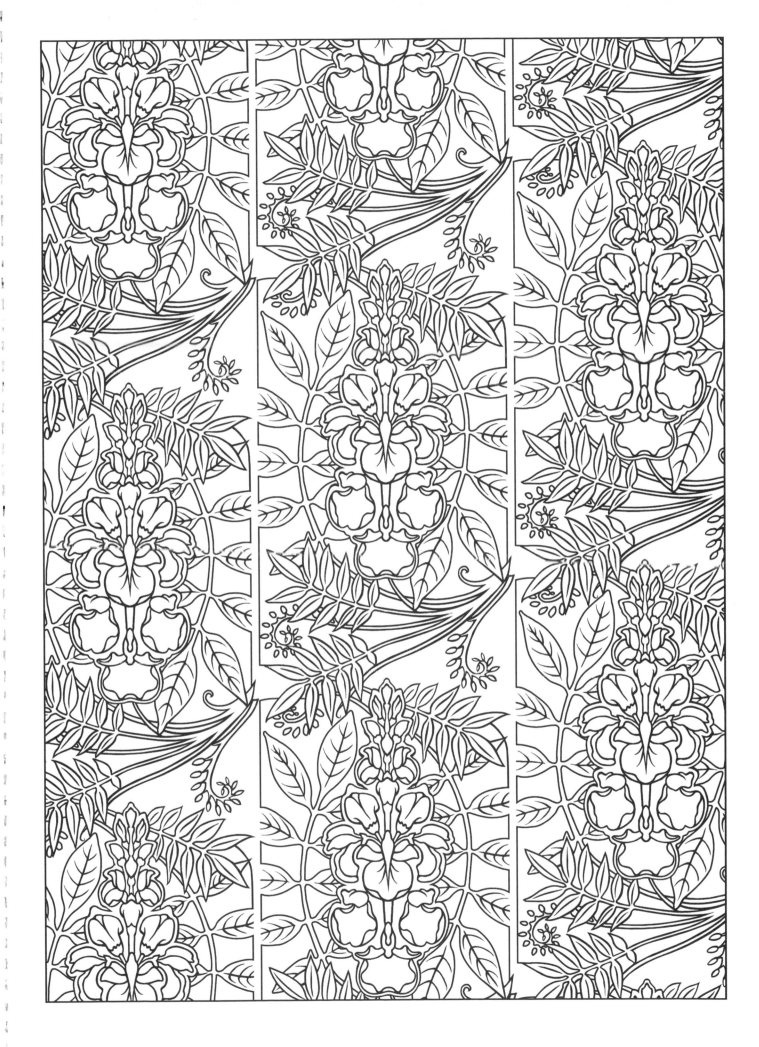

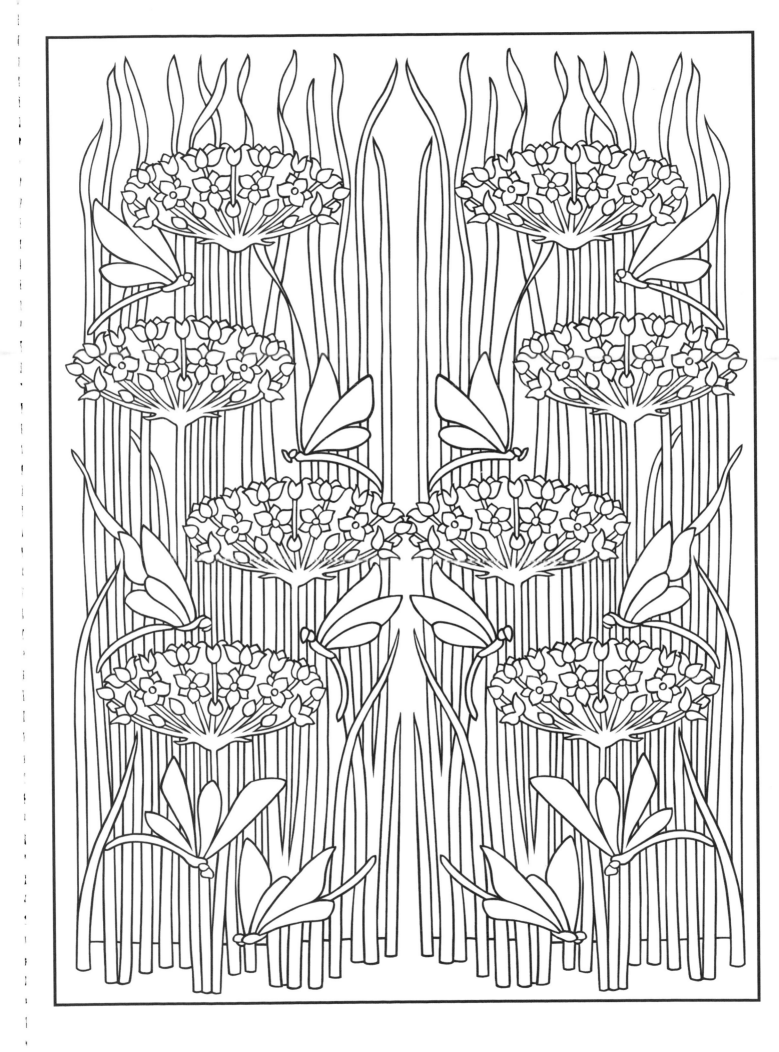

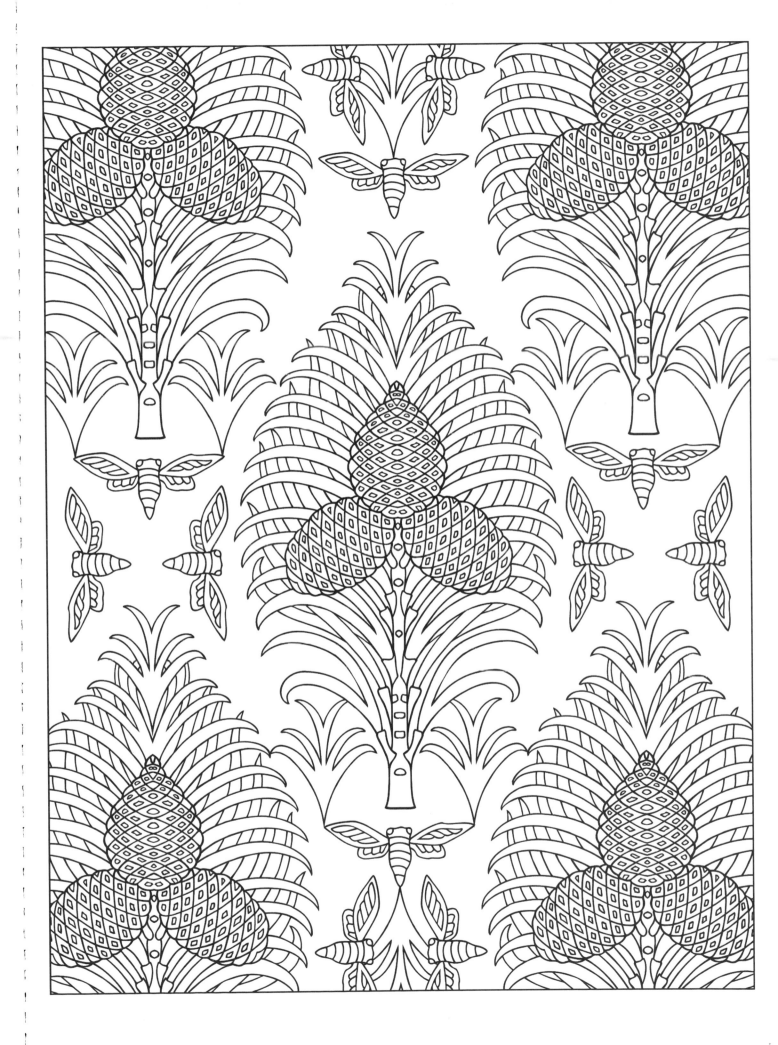

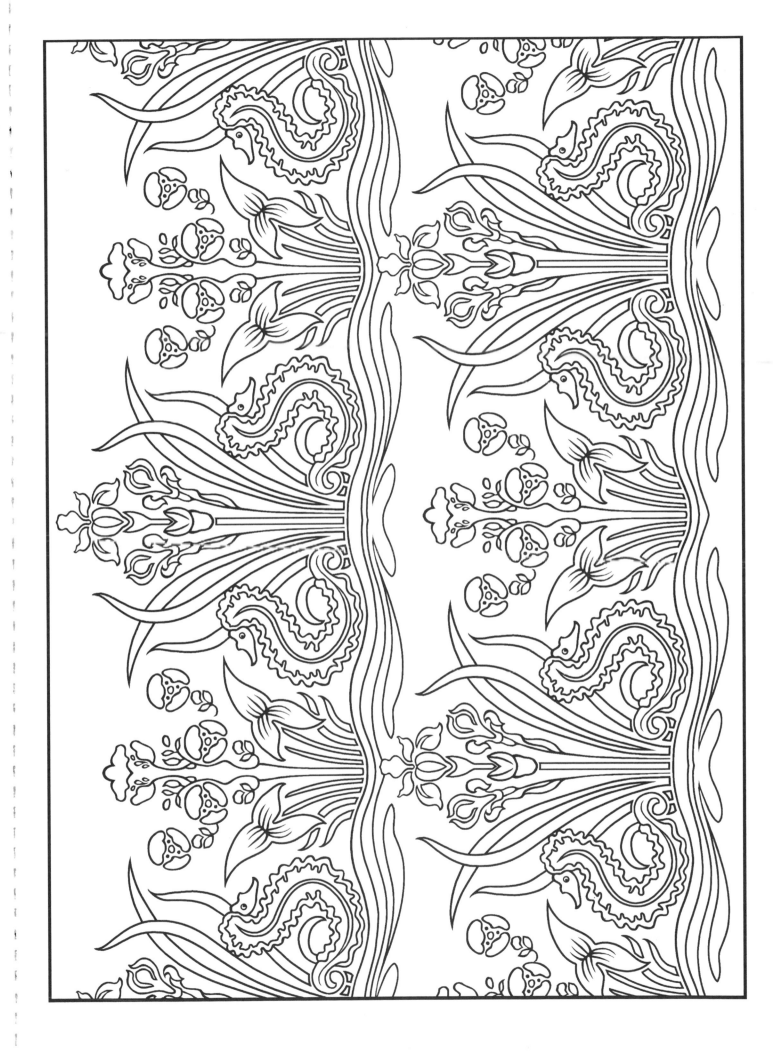

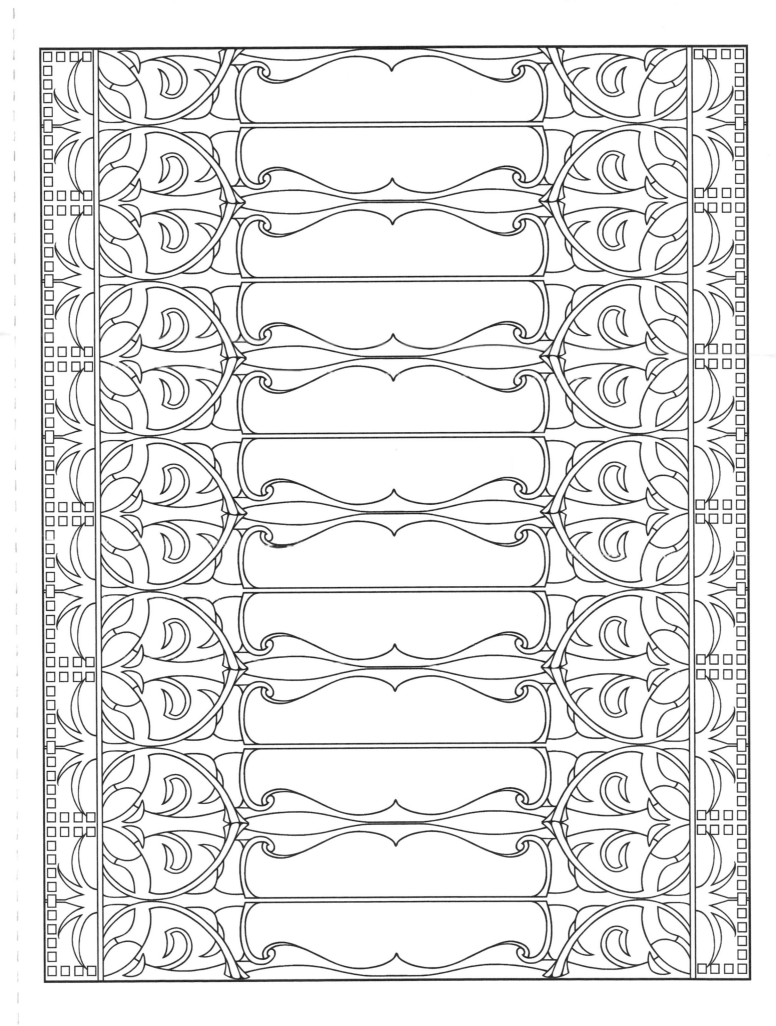

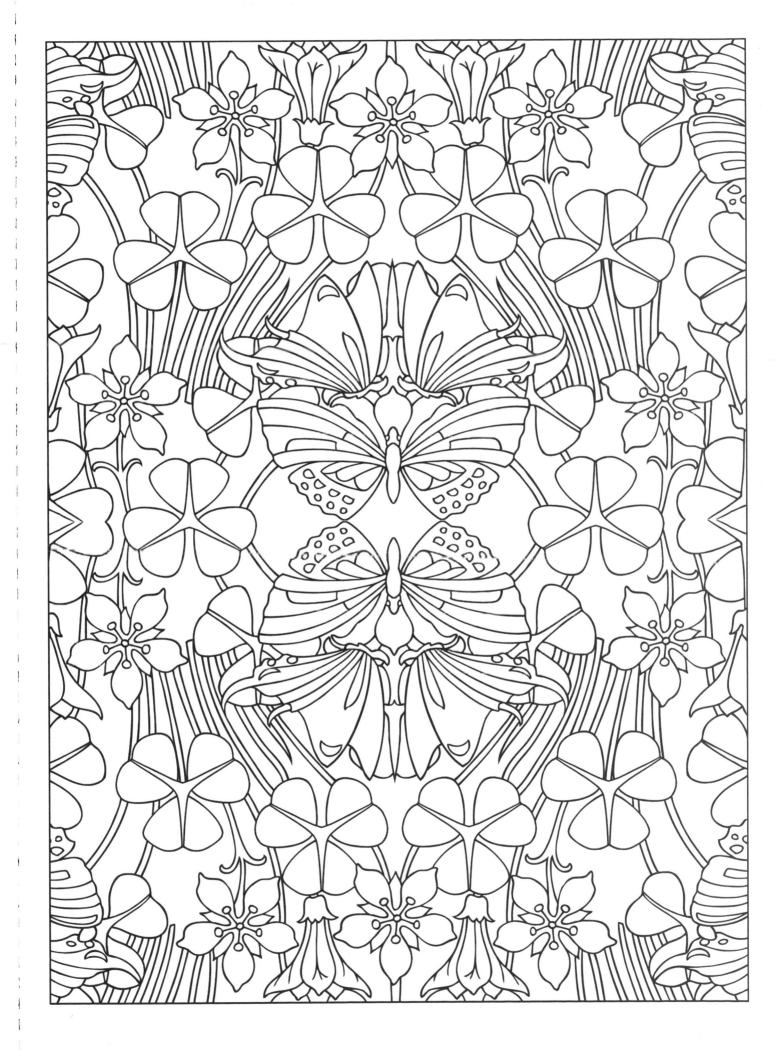

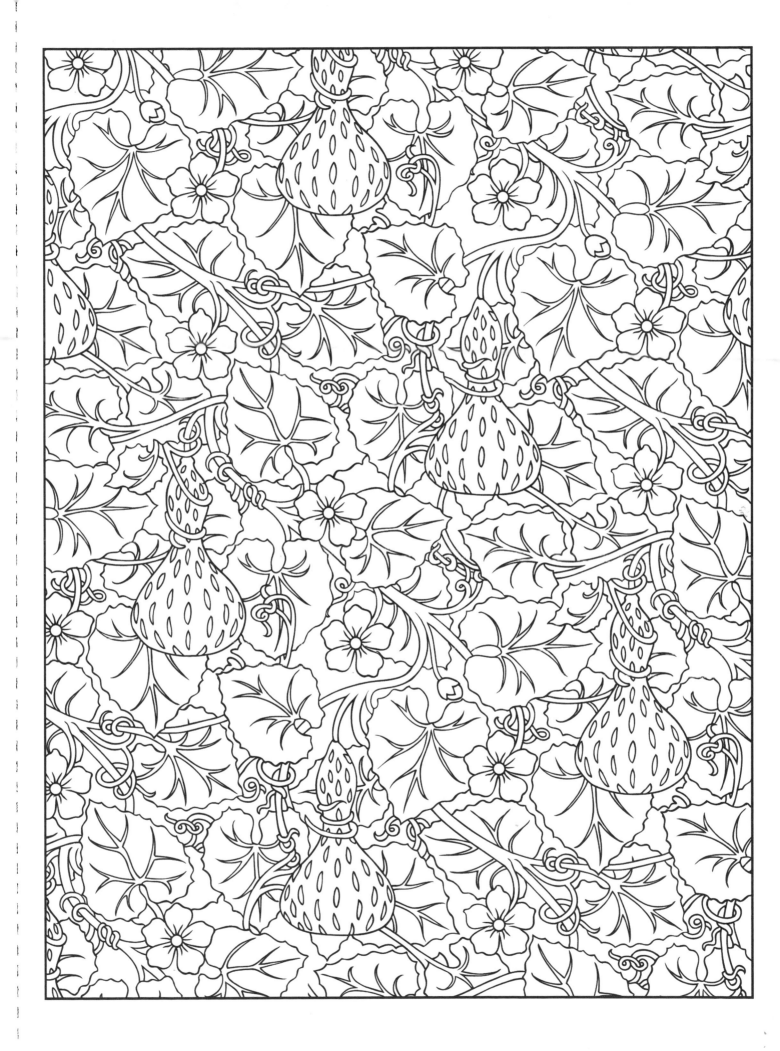

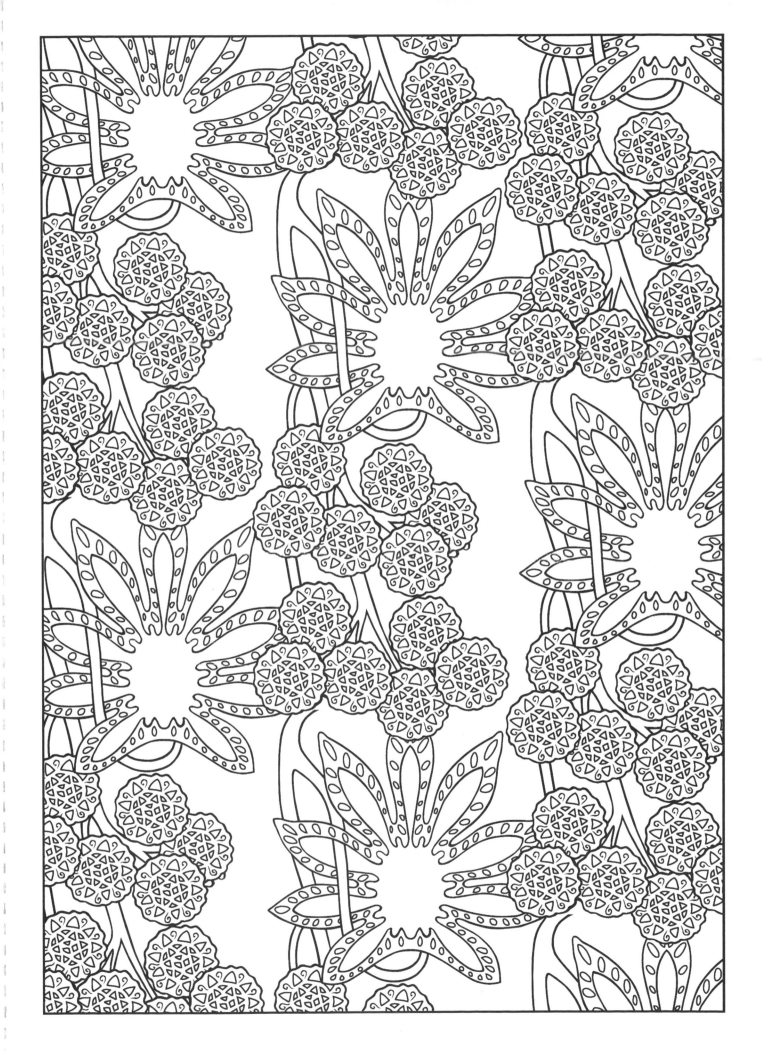

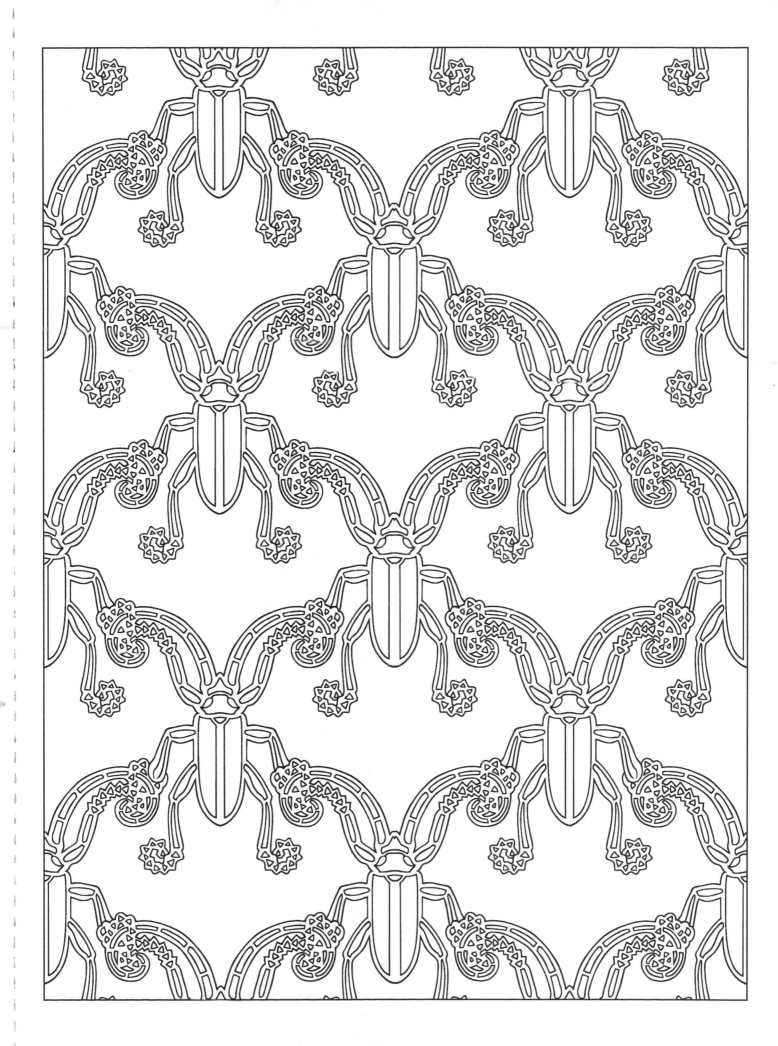

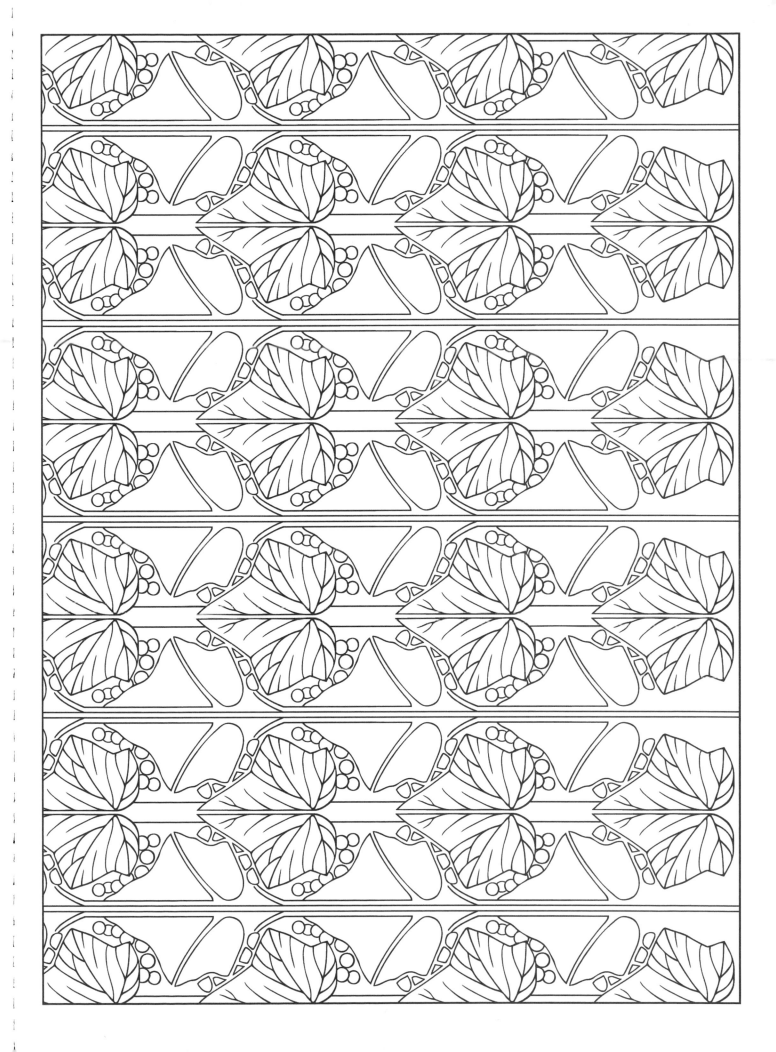

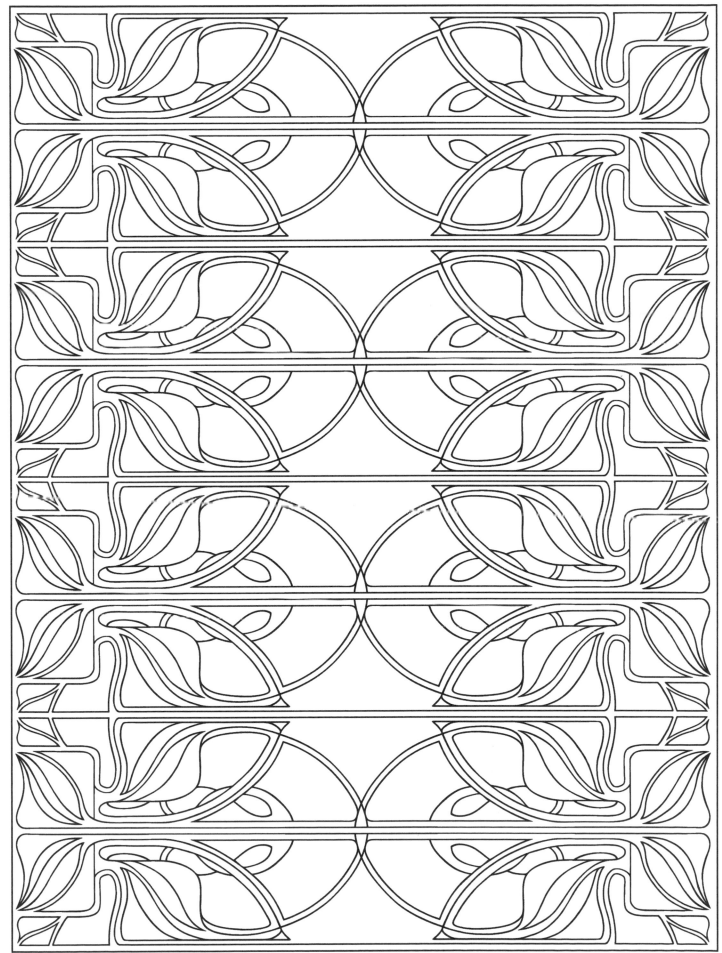

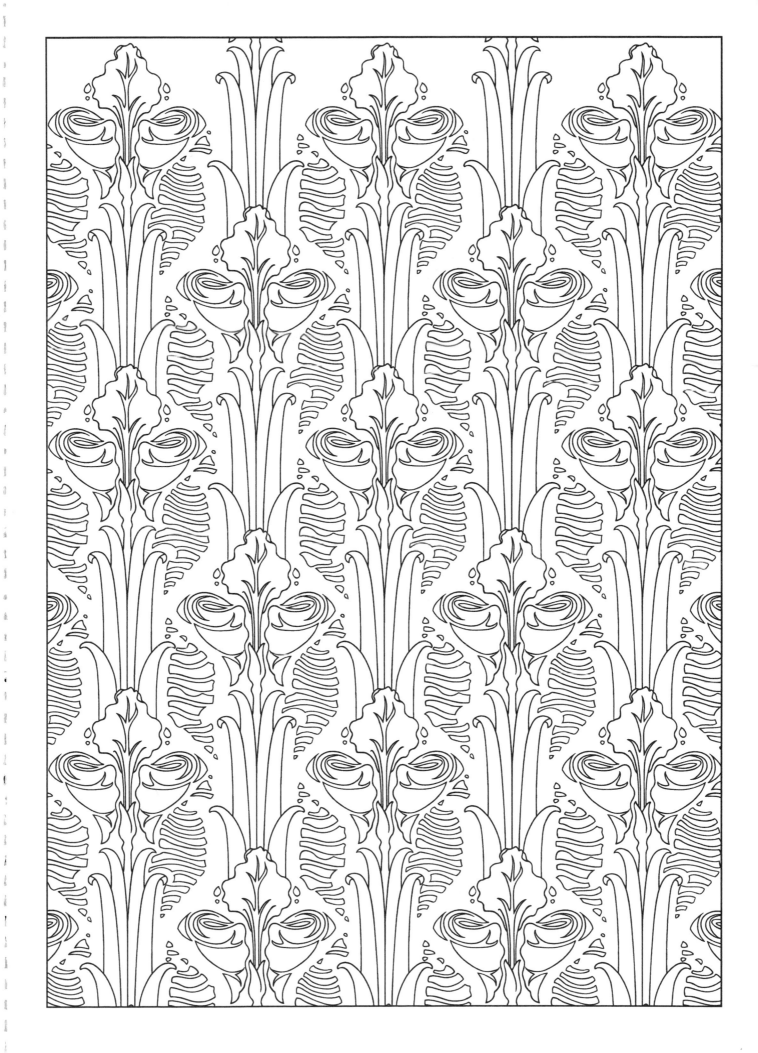

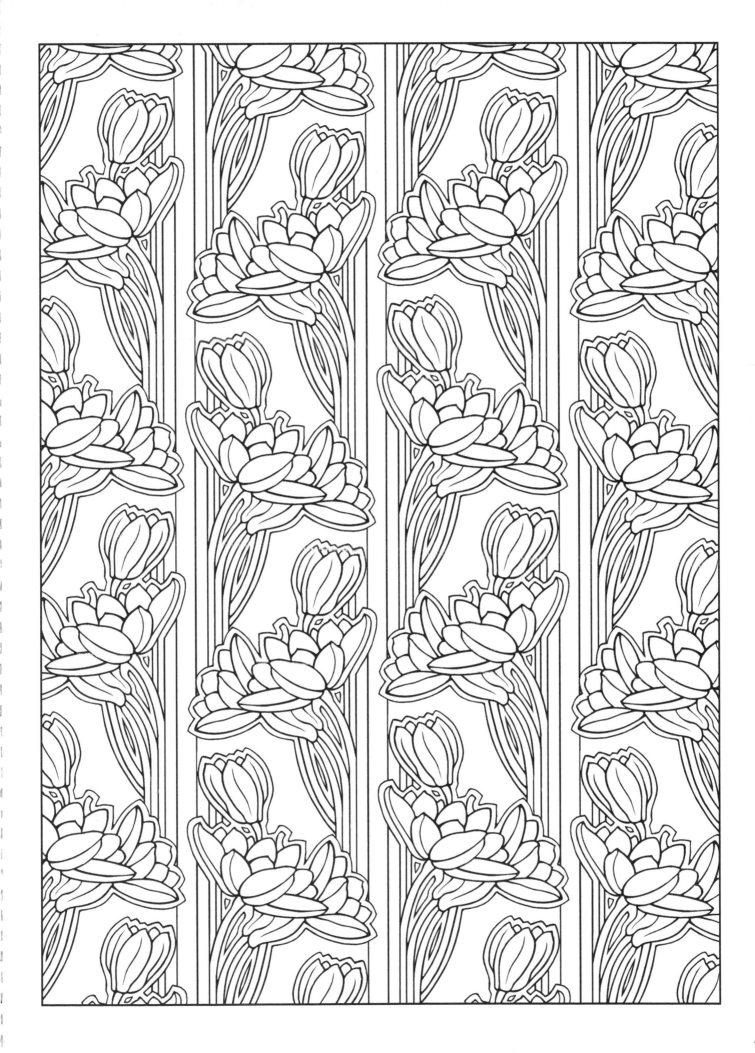

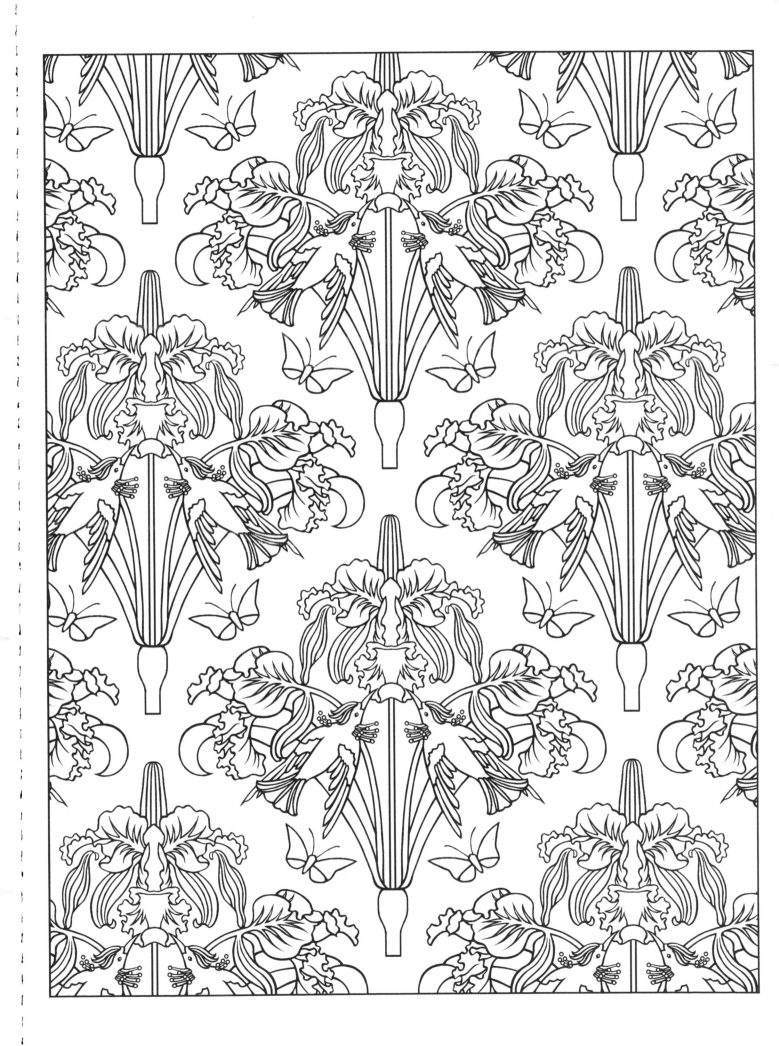

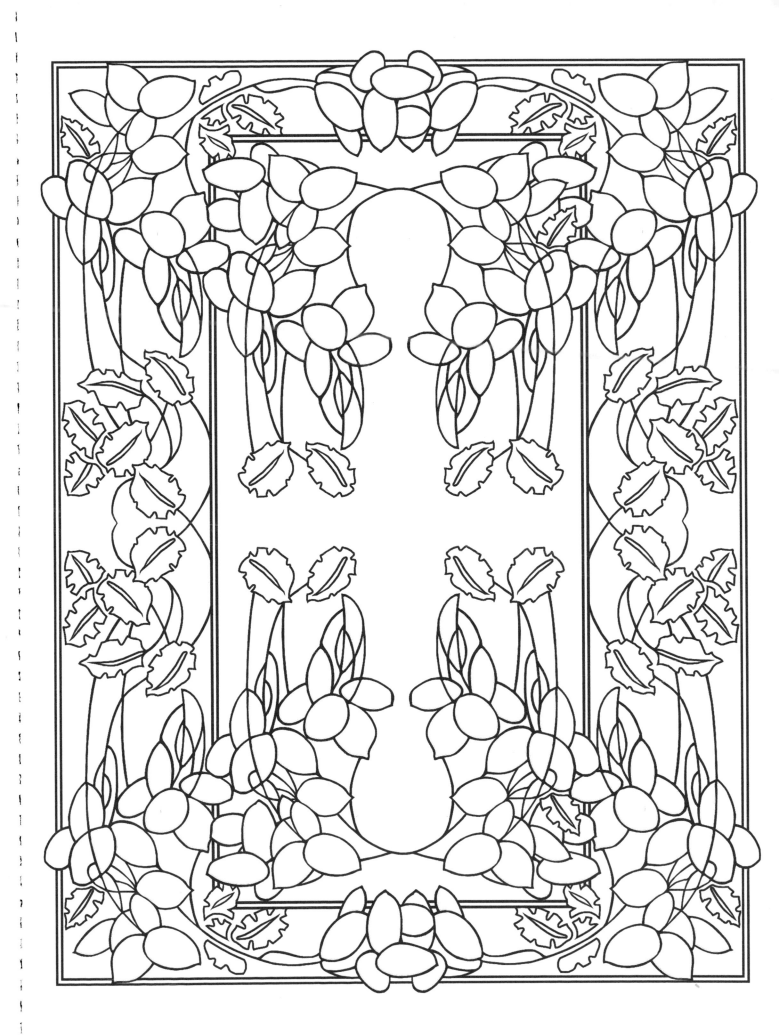

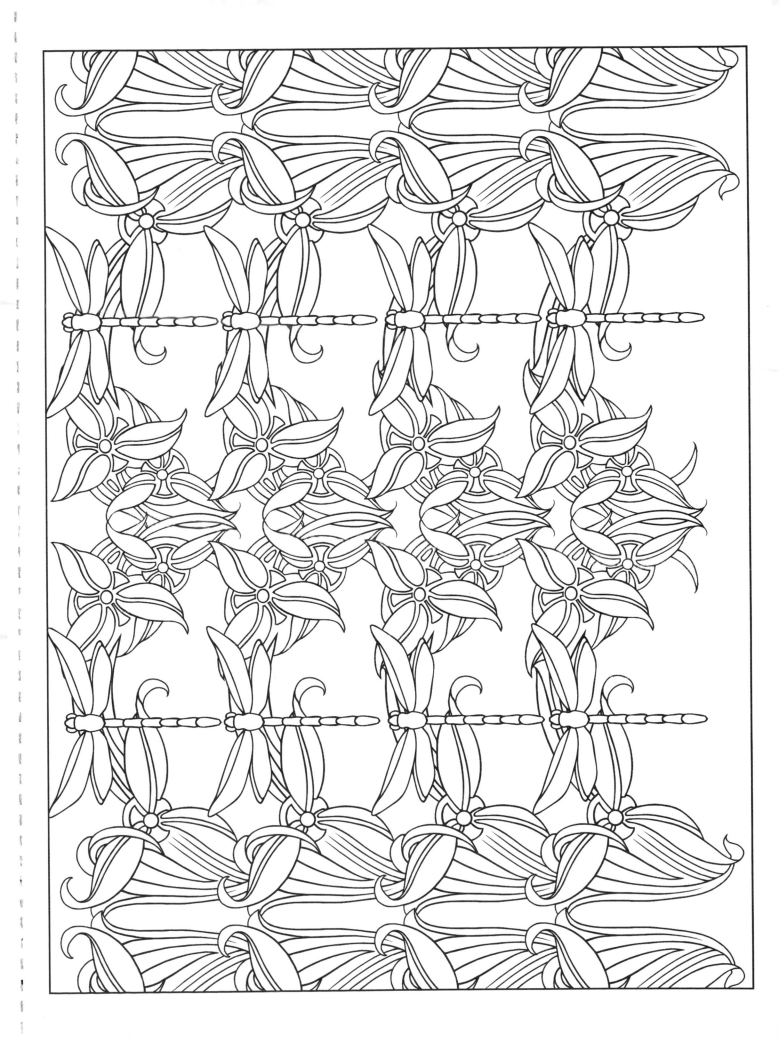

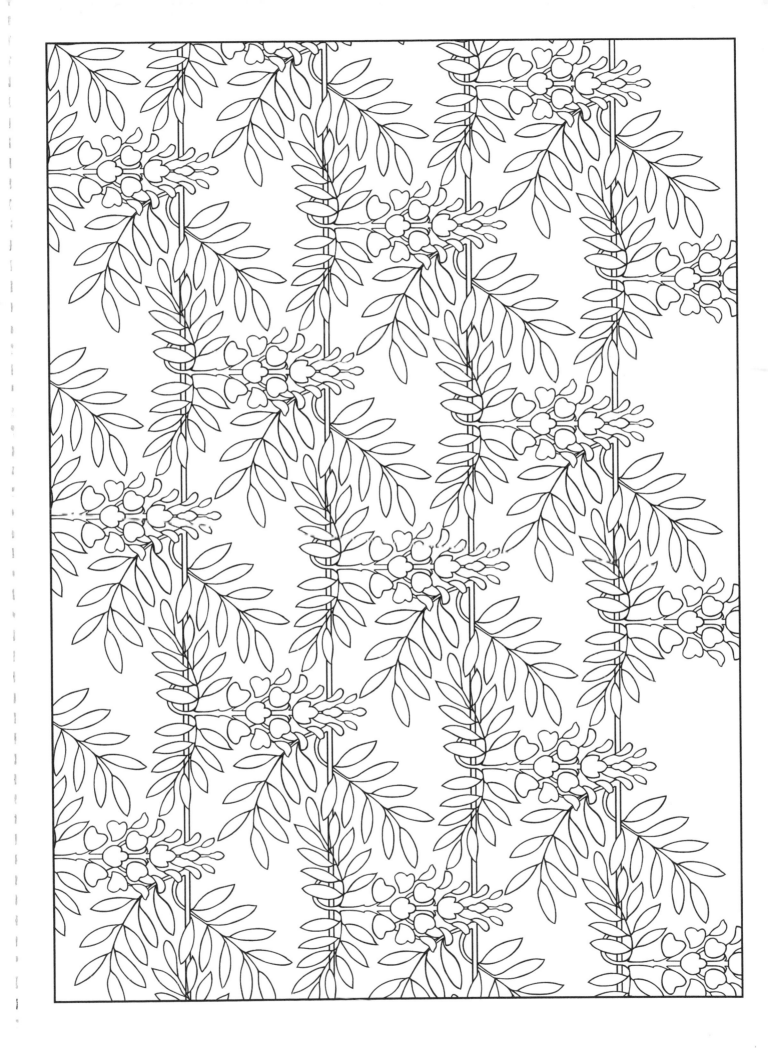

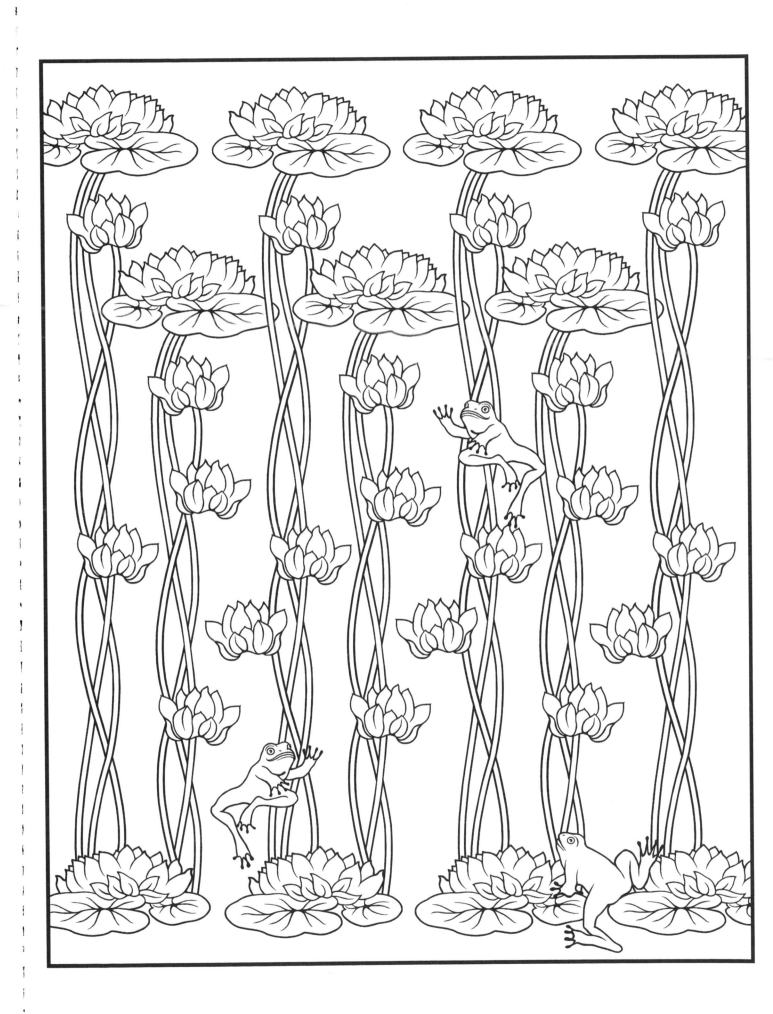

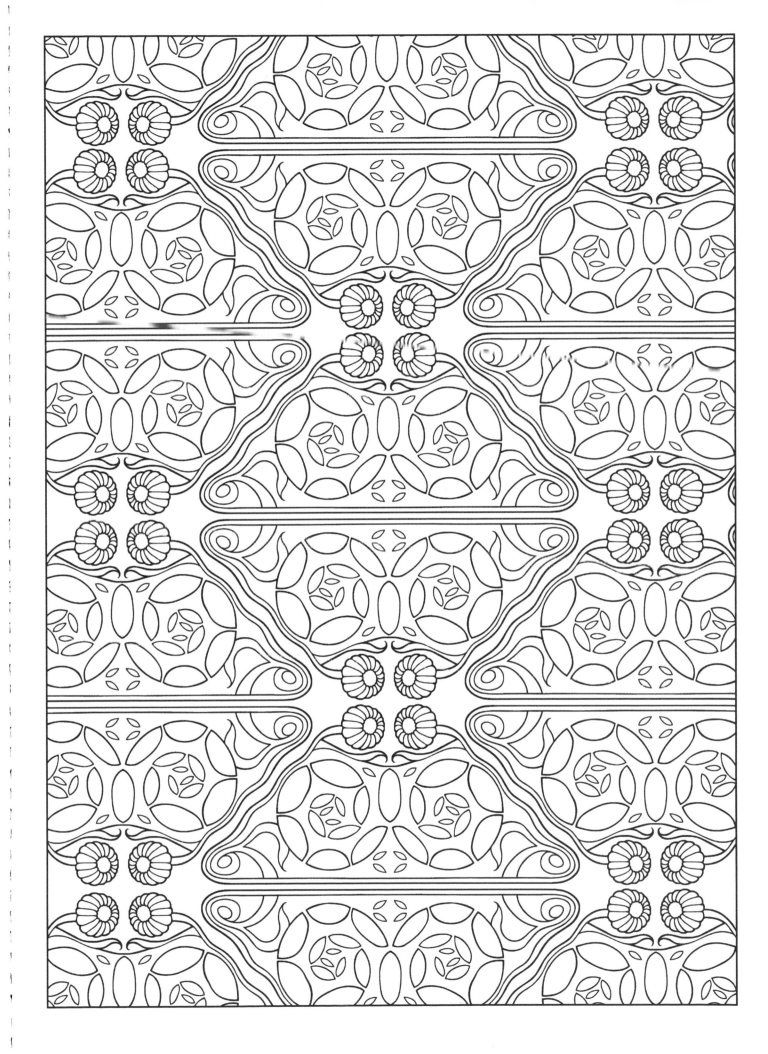

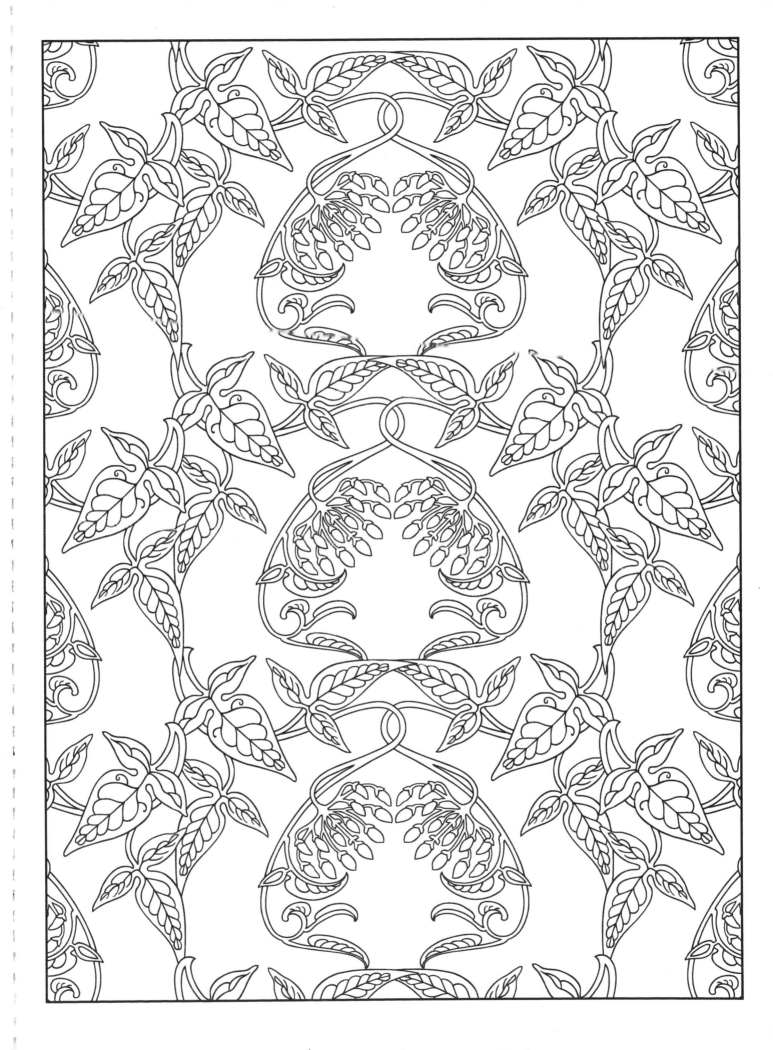

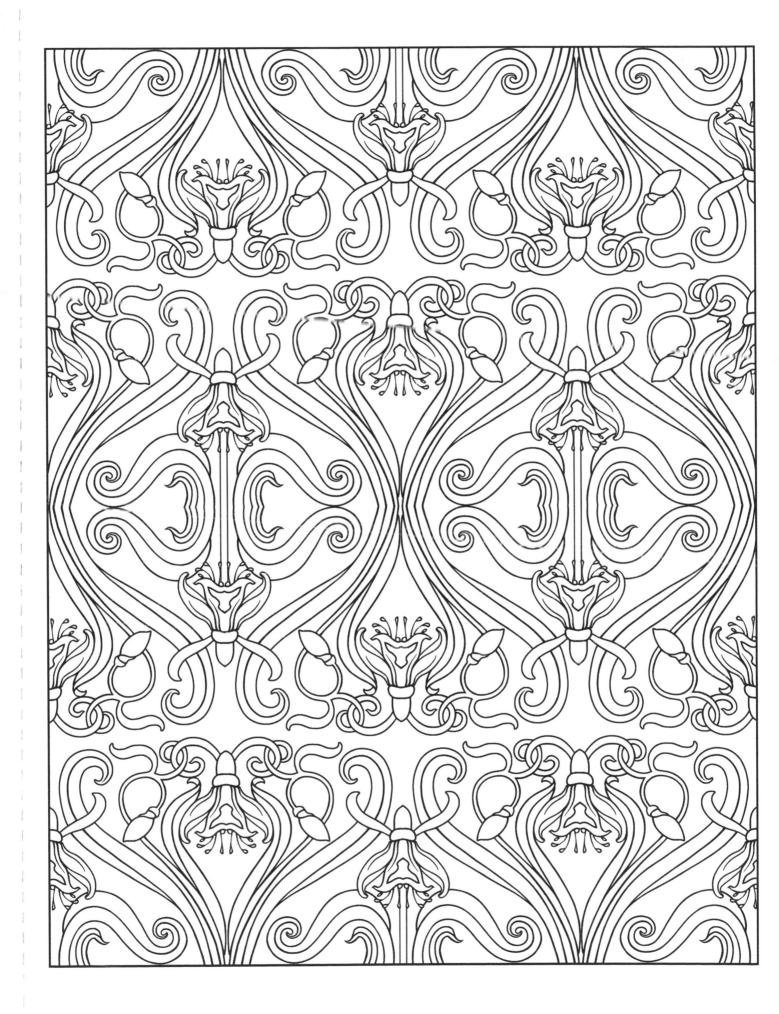

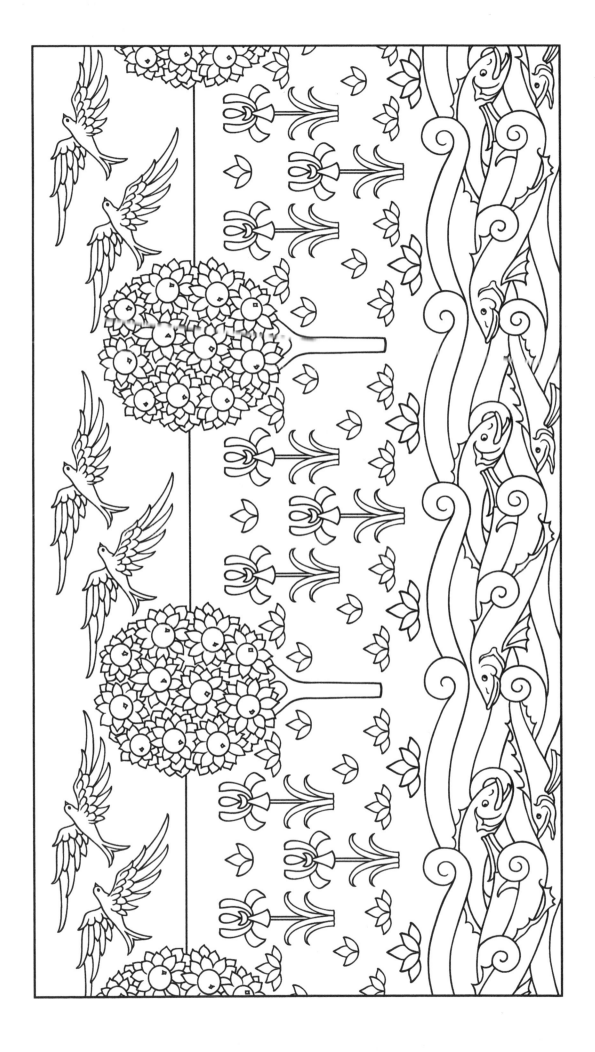

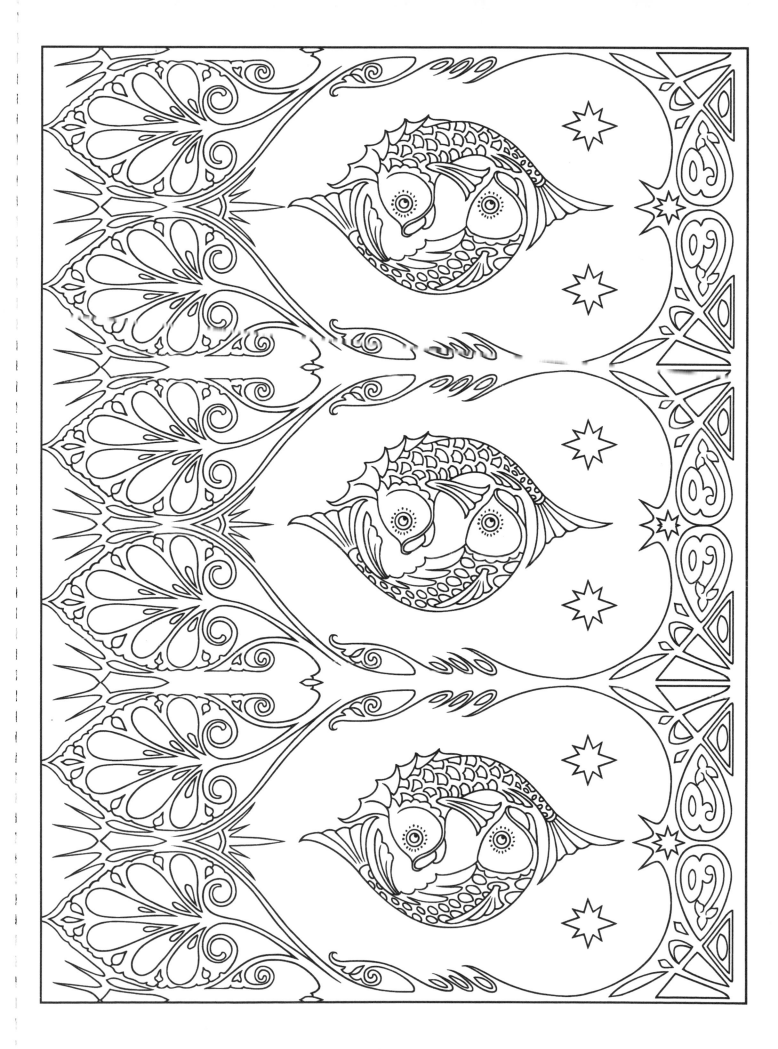

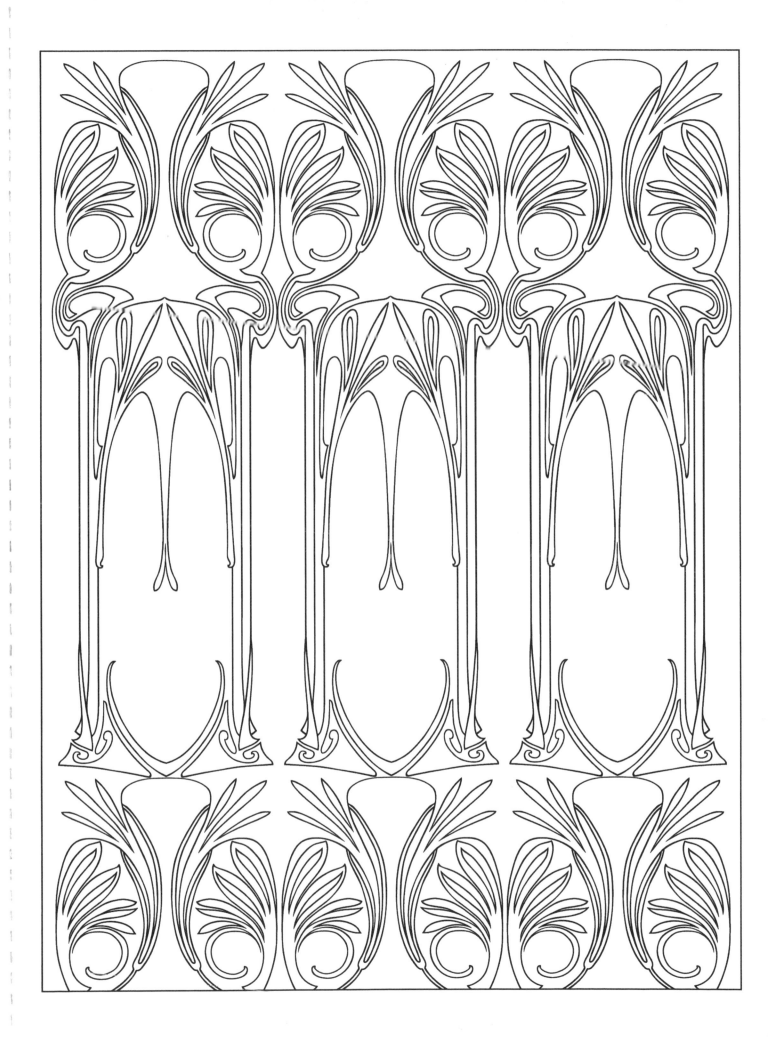

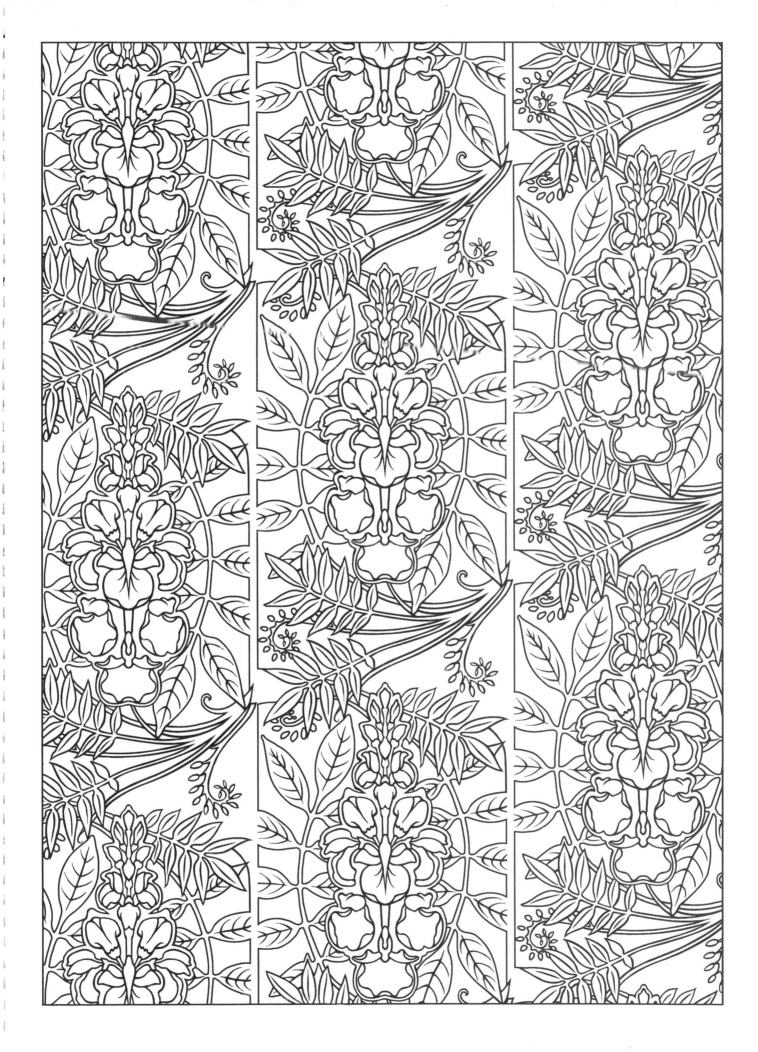

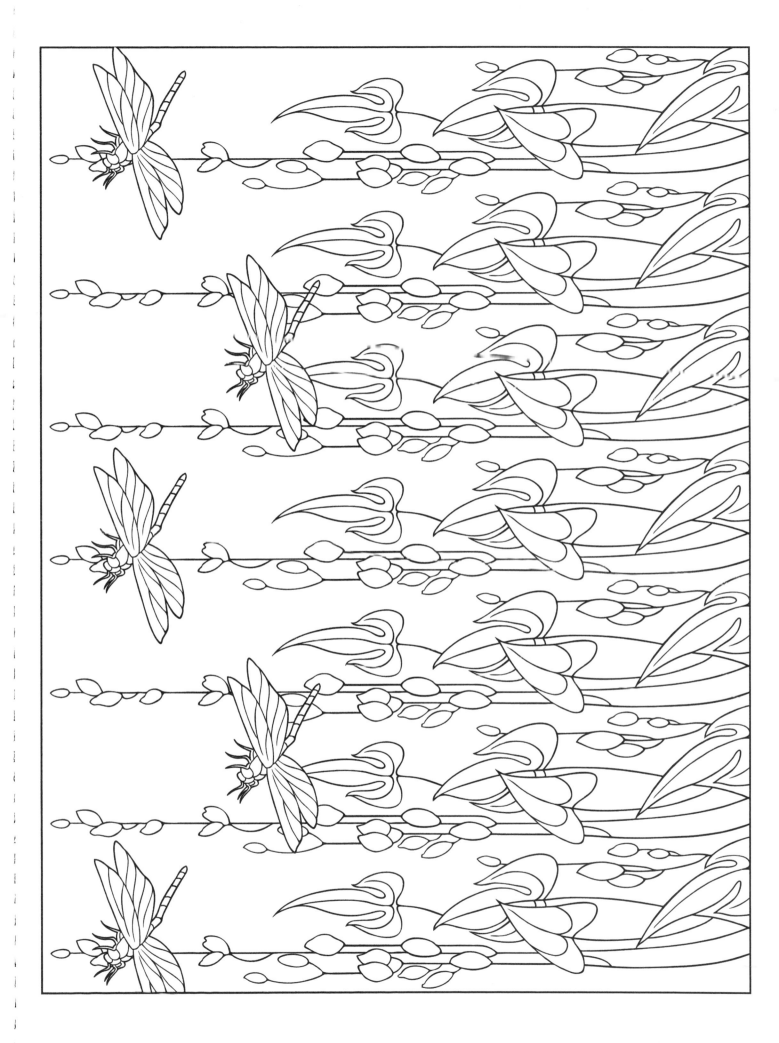